Praise for *A Fierce Belief in Miracles*

"*A Fierce Belief in Miracles* is the compelling and moving story of Anne Heck's quest to understand and transform the scrambled pieces of her heart and soul in the aftermath of sexual violence. Through her fearless exploration of healing modalities over two decades and her determination to embrace the arduous journey and its mysteries, she bestows a gift of hope. Heck's story of her path to meaning, truth, and transformative integration is an important contribution to the growing body of literature on sexual violence—its complex impact on individuals and society."

—Nancy Venable Raine,
author of *After Silence: Rape and My Journey Back*

"Anne gives us the courage to trust that the unconventional path to healing might just be the greatest gift of our lives."

—Amy B. Scher, author of *This Is How I Save My Life*
and *How to Heal Yourself When No One Else Can*

A Fierce
Belief in
Miracles

A Fierce Belief in Miracles

My Journey from Rape to Healing and Wholeness

Anne Reeder Heck

She Writes Press, a BookSparks imprint
A Division of SparkPointStudio, LLC.

Published 2020
Printed in the United States of America

Print ISBN: 978-1-63152-749-4
E-ISBN: 978-1-63152-750-0
Library of Congress Control Number: 2020905950

For information, address:
She Writes Press
1569 Solano Ave #546
Berkeley, CA 94707

She Writes Press is a division of SparkPoint Studio, LLC.

Names and identifying characteristics have been changed to protect the privacy of certain individuals.

Disclaimer

This book shares the story of the author's personal healing and spiritual development. It is not written with the intent that others should follow any of the protocols described within. This book is not intended as a substitute for grief or trauma counseling or the advice of a qualified spiritual, mental health, or wellness practitioner. Readers should consult their own health professionals and spiritual advisors about matters relating to physical, mental, and spiritual health.

For my parents, Jane and Paul Reeder,
who raised me to know I could accomplish anything,

and for my grandmother, Virginia Rose Hechter Reeder,
who inspired me to write

Contents

PART TWO

PART THREE

Foreword

Many survivors of sexual assault are fearful of telling their stories. Anne Heck is not that kind of survivor. And this book is more than the story of her rape. It's the story of her unexpected path to healing.

Despite her science education and trust in modern medicine, Anne placed her faith in an unknown and often mysterious process that led her step by step into unfamiliar territory. Unknowingly, she was traveling the path of the wounded healer, a heroic journey that pushed her far beyond the edges of her comfort zone. On this path she met allies, guides, and teachers who helped her rediscover strength, resilience, and wholeness.

Anne and I came to know one another when she enrolled in my online class, Medicine Dolls: How to Make Healing Dolls for Yourself. In this class, participants explore personal stories and a range of perceptions and emotions—and, in doing so, reach a deeper level of self-understanding. Anne jumped right into doll making with commitment and a playful approach. She discovered that her dolls had personalities and voices and would play an integral role in her healing.

By choosing an unconventional path to healing, Anne initiated the creation of what is called a "mandorla" for her life experience. As a visual symbol, a mandorla is an almond-shaped area created when two identical circles overlap so that the center of each touches the edge of the other. This ancient symbol of illumination represents a sacred space—a space where we begin to understand that we have the ability to take what we believed was a curse and transform it into a powerful medicine for the soul. Jungian analyst Robert Johnson describes a mandorla as "a creative synthesis of partnership, conflict resolution, healing, and peacemaking."

Anne's miracle, her personal mandorla, involved experiencing the tensions within her body, mind, and spirit, then moving the pain, beauty, and terror into a space where opposites could be resolved. This unconventional journey worked its magic—it facilitated deep healing; brought wisdom, meaning, and joy; and allowed Anne to discover and integrate her authentic healing powers.

This experience changed Anne from a victim of rape into an author, speaker, healer, and artist who dedicates her work to helping women connect with their personal power and speak their truth.

I invite you to read and allow Anne's story to work its magic and miracles on you.

It did on me.

—Barb Kobe, author of *The Healing Doll Way: A Guided Process Creating Art Dolls for Self-Discovery, Awareness, and Transformation.*
More information is at www.barbkobe.com and www.healingdollway.com.

Sharing My Story

*Listen. Really listen. There is a wisdom inside of you
that goes beyond what you think you know.*
— Joanna Garritano, MD

Healing from trauma is a gutsy endeavor. It cannot be approached with logic, nor with expectations about a quick fix. Healing requires us to dive in, to be fully present with the discomfort and ugliness, to show compassion for ourselves, and to listen intently. This has been my life's work.

As much as I wanted to box up the pain and tuck it away, I couldn't. My physical body and my spirit kept whispering that all was not well. And the way to get through or beyond what felt broken was not always clear. Listening—really listening—required a steep learning curve. It's still a work in progress.

Mine has been an unconventional path to healing—a path I never expected to take. But in retrospect, I wouldn't have done anything differently. As I tally the gifts among the hardships, I find there are many.

I spent years browsing libraries and later the Internet to find a true story of someone who had navigated their way to wholeness after rape—a story that could give me hope in what sometimes seemed a hopeless search. Now, years after the trauma, I've been called to share my story.

I wish you gentleness and ease on your journey. With this book, I plant a seed of intention that you will discover what you seek.

PART ONE

Prayer

My Trek 400 road bike—bright red—leaned against the brick wall outside my apartment, its tires freshly inflated, water bottles filled. An hour earlier, I'd climbed out of bed as the summer sun crept down the wall of my bedroom. The blue skies were already deepening in color, and I smiled inwardly, eager to breeze down the road with the sun and wind against my skin. As I enjoyed a hearty breakfast of French toast and fruit, I pored over maps and considered where I wanted to go.

Summer meant time off from teaching, and after nine months of lesson plans and teenagers, I relished the freedom from tight schedules and the solitude of being on two wheels surrounded by rolling hills. Living on the northern edge of Manassas, Virginia, just thirty miles west of the nation's capital, I often sought to escape the traffic and ride my bike in the quiet countryside.

It was July 26, 1990—a Thursday. As I washed and put away the breakfast dishes, I planned the route. Just three miles north was Manassas National Battlefield Park, site of the Civil War battles of Bull Run. Heading past the park, then slightly west, would deliver me to scenic and gentle terrain—grassy fields and a chance to enjoy turning my pedals while taking in the beauty.

Before getting on my bike, I often considered my hopes and dreams or a problem I wanted to solve. Then I'd state a wish or intention—you could call it a prayer—that I'd take into my wheel-turning meditation. This deliberate practice focused my mind as I sank into riding rhythm.

As a busy twenty-six-year-old, I didn't practice prayer; I wasn't convinced that it accomplished much, but I didn't want to discount it altogether. I was intrigued with spiritual mystery and the possibility hidden in seeds of personal intention. For a moment, stating my wish, I could indulge in what my child self had known as magic.

As a youngster, with my eyes closed, I'd gently blow on a white dandelion puffball and make a wish as its feathery seeds dispersed across lush grass and green clover. These fluffy grains of desire floated away on my breath, along with any awareness of the intention I'd just set in motion. The idea that my wish might be realized as a result of my "prayer" wasn't part of my consciousness then. And I still don't fully understand what happens within me, or out in the world, when I make a wish. I do know, though, that it involves both agency and help.

Donning my favorite blue biking shorts and shirt, I zeroed out the mileage on my bike computer and tucked a snack bar into the pouch under my saddle. I'd ridden the area west of the battlefields a few times; my cycling friend Ted and I had taken several spins on the quiet roads in horse country. Some twenty miles away, in Middleburg, was a café where I could enjoy a tasty lunch as a midday reward. Ted and I had stopped at this quaint small-town bakery on the Bike MS ride in May.

The place had been easy to spot that day; as we approached

Middleburg, a line of hungry lycra-clad cyclists, helmets in hand, spilled out the door waiting for service. The food was well worth the wait. The menu, written in chalk on large blackboards just inside the door, highlighted the day's specials—chicken salad sandwiches and the bakery's signature cow puddle cookies. Nearly everything tastes good when you've been cycling all day, but the café was a special spot, and a perfect direction for the day's ride. I'd find some back roads to get there.

Ted and I had met on Bike MS, a two-day ride of a hundred miles through scenic countryside, with crowds of cyclists camped out in fields overnight and a large truck carrying our gear. At one of the morning rest stations on our first day, I rode into a church parking lot where several plastic tables brimmed with Dixie water cups, fig bars, and fruit. Two cyclists stood to the side, leaning on their bikes and cheering those who were slowing to stop.

"Five-eleven!"—my MS ride number—they bellowed as I coasted to a stop. Ted and a fellow rider, Greg, introduced themselves as I dismounted. This enthusiastic duo was present at many of the upcoming rest stops, and we wove in and out of each other's company all day. We soon knew each other as friends.

Ted was in tip-top physical shape, with ebony skin, a broad deep-dimpled smile, and bright eyes. He worked for the Environmental Protection Agency and was an animated fun-hog whose energy was infectious. I was quickly drawn to his vibrant nature. In the coming weeks, I joined the EPA softball team, and a bunch of us played games in the evenings on the grassy lawn of the National Mall.

Ted relished a physical challenge. I longed to join him and Greg on an eighty-mile cycling adventure they planned one

Friday, from DC to Skyline Drive. But school was still in session, and the best I could do was get up early that morning and fix them a huge pancake breakfast before I headed off to work.

"There are gonna be some 'Oh Nelly' hills!" Ted said as he devoured blueberry buckwheat cakes and gulped orange juice. "Oh Nellys" were the really steep ones. "We're gonna miss ya, girl." I helped pump tires and fill water bottles, then sent them on their way and cycled off to work. That evening, I drove with Ted's wife to the couple's mountain cabin, where we all shared a meal, played board games, and talked and laughed the evening away.

Riding with Ted never failed to entertain and inspire. He'd often coach me from behind. "Pump those pipes, girl!" His "Oh Nellys" made us both laugh. At rest stops, we told stories and laughed even more, with Ted usually initiating both.

As I got to know Ted better, my admiration grew for his authenticity and confidence. He seemed to have an inner grounding spot that strengthened him—a place of wisdom from which he could act and speak with clarity. He expressed himself with passion and a fullness of heart. His self-assured demeanor, for me, exemplified faith—though in what, I wasn't sure.

What struck me was that he seemed to trust that something—God or some higher power—always had his back. As a child, I'd felt that same confident knowing and taken it completely for granted. But in my life in Manassas, I felt disconnected from this sense of inner certainty and wanted to recover it.

Ted told stories of miracles with such conviction that even my scientific skeptical mind wanted to believe them. He knew a woman, he said, who'd traveled to Africa as a missionary. There, she had no money for gas, so she said to God, "If you brought me over here to work for you, you have to provide." In her months in

Prayer

Africa, she drove her little beat-up car from the country to the city for supplies, never filling the tank, yet the gas gauge always registered full.

So, on the morning of July 26, as I prepared for my solo daytime ride, I thought about Ted. I considered my own spiritual search, how I'd questioned my beliefs in college and then landed in Manassas with a new job, new people—a new life. All positive transitions, but still unsettling. As if tossed into unfamiliar water, I was floating in its depths trying to find ballast. I so desired Ted's confidence and faith: something to believe in deeply and unequivocally, to *trust*. So I went seeking on that warm summer day in 1990. That morning, I said a prayer that I would somehow secure such trust—find my own inner faith. I had no idea what might be required of me to grow into the knowing I craved.

I tucked my map into my handlebar bag, hopped on my bike, and headed north. The roads were busy as I pedaled through the edge of town, but blessedly less so as I passed the panorama of the battlefields. The sun was warm. I felt strong and satisfied with my intent for the day, as I often had as a kid.

Back then, I'd been a curious explorer. On my bike I explored our neighborhood's every road and driveway, seeking connections and shortcuts. I spent countless hours climbing trees and studying the snakes and insects, plants and trees that filled our seven-acre property in rural Ohio. I often left the house at the first rumbles of thunder before a storm, looking forward to a long hike in the rain. And always, I did my invincible tomboy best to keep up with my two brothers.

"I dare you to ride your bike down it," my older brother had said one summer evening when I was seven years old. We were standing at the top of the steep, grassy hill in our front yard.

In a flash, I jumped on my tiny blue Schwinn. For reasons I

can't remember, the bike's chain had been removed, making the pedal brakes useless. I pushed off and screamed with glee for a bit before realizing I couldn't stop.

A voice inside me whispered, *Jump now*. Without hesitation, and knowing I'd be okay, I wrenched my body away from the bike, hitting the grass in a rough landing, just feet from the asphalt road below.

My next memory was waking in our porcelain bathtub. Mom was watching me from a wooden stool. "Are you okay?" she asked, looking into my face and down at my scraped, bruised body.

"Yes," I said, "I'm okay."

That wasn't the last time my bicycle would take me on a painful journey. Nor would it be the last time I'd listen to an inner voice and trust that it would guide me.

2

Impact

On the morning of July 26, I had passed the battlefields and was about twenty minutes into my ride when I came upon a gravel road that I didn't remember seeing the last time I'd taken this route. I stopped and checked the map. The road appeared to be the right direction, and I'd end up connecting with the road to Middleburg. I could almost smell the sweetness of the bakery at lunchtime. I headed down the gravel road.

Immediately I sensed that something wasn't right—a strong inner knowing that I shouldn't take the gravel road I'd just turned onto. Though my mind argued for a moment, I turned my bike around and headed back to the paved road. I'd find another path to my destination, and hopefully one that wasn't gravel.

Moments after I started back down the paved road, I felt a hesitation. I stopped and checked the map again.

A voice inside my head prodded: *Take that gravel road.*

The gravel road does appear to be the most direct route to the bakery, I thought, affirming the voice.

But it also feels foreboding, my mind countered.

Still, there was a feeling about the gravel road that I couldn't shake—almost a curiosity. *I wonder what I'd find if I rode that way?*

Despite some inner resistance, I decided not to question the choice any longer. *I'll test out the gravel road and see where it goes.*

The gravel was hardly enjoyable, given the narrow tires of my road bike, and after a few minutes of riding, I dismounted and decided to walk for a bit.

The dry, desolate road was bordered only by mature forest. Fine dust hung in the air, the way it sometimes does above a gravel road on a hot day. The sun had climbed high enough into the hazy sky that it'd begun to bake my head, so I removed my bike helmet and walked with it tucked under my arm.

Not far into my walk, a red car came toward me on the road. I didn't pay it much attention; my thoughts were on getting past this gravel portion and reaching smooth pavement again. I wondered how far I'd need to walk on this rough, loose surface in the hot sun.

The car passed slowly, creating dust. The driver, his window down, was looking directly at me. He stopped his car behind me, which I thought unusual, and I heard him step out of the car and begin to walk hurriedly toward me. I turned to face him.

"I need help with directions," he said. He sounded agitated and in a hurry.

He's fortunate I travel with a map. I'm not entirely certain where I am, but we can likely figure it out for both of us. Without hesitation, I turned to pull my map out of the sleeve on my bike bag. When I turned back around, his fist was in my face.

The impact was strong, direct. I could feel my teeth thrust back and my mouth suddenly swollen. Blood trickled down my chin onto my favorite blue cycling shirt. The man grabbed my arm and twisted it behind my back. With his other hand he grabbed my bike and threw it over an embankment. Holding tight on my twisted arm, he pushed me from behind into the woods.

I felt myself float away and begin to experience the scene from somewhere outside my physical body. I felt strangely disconnected from what was happening; even my breath seemed to come from somewhere other than my lungs. *I'm gonna live through this. I'm gonna live through this.* The phrase became my focus, my silent mantra.

"What's your name?" he asked.

"Cindy," I lied, recalling a friend from graduate school who was spunky and strong.

His grip on my arm was already tight, and he twisted it further, forcing me to my knees. He released my arm and stood over me. I looked up and saw the details of his face for the first time. He was pale with a slender nose and beady, desperate eyes. His front teeth were crooked, one overlapping the other, his lips tightly pursed. With dirty-blond unkempt hair and wrinkled clothes, he looked as if he had been driving all night.

His T-shirt was moist and stained with sweat, and from my position on the ground, he seemed large, his torso broad and his bulky abdomen extending over his faded jeans. Everything had become silent; even my breath seemed to have stopped.

"Stay on your knees," he ordered. He unzipped his jeans. His pudgy hands pulled out a small, limp penis.

I felt myself spinning, a dizzy sensation that came with hampered breathing.

"Suck on it!"

I wanted to spit, to bite it, anything but that. The blood dribbled from my mouth. I could feel my broken teeth hanging by threads, but I didn't dare anger him. I was intent on getting away with my life. I put my mouth tentatively on the piece.

He promptly pulled away and got behind me, roughly yanking down my shorts and shoving himself into me. I closed my eyes. *I'm gonna live through this. I'm gonna live through this.*

He ejaculated. *God, help me live through this,* I prayed.

"If you tell anyone about this, I'll kill you," he threatened. I didn't doubt it. Then he turned and ran back to the road, to his red car, and sped away, leaving a cloud of dust and devastation behind him.

I don't remember how I arrived back at the roadside. I had a hard time focusing and hardly felt my limbs. Amazingly, an old blue pickup truck drove up at the moment I came out of the trees. No doubt I was a frightening image, with blood covering my face and chest. The driver helped me into his truck, pulled a crumpled plaid wool blanket from behind his seat, and wrapped it around my shoulders. He drove me to a nearby fire and rescue station, which was equipped with an ambulance. I was hastened into the vehicle, placed on a wheeled stretcher, and asked if I needed oxygen.

"No, thank you," I said automatically. "I can breathe on my own."

I don't remember breathing, however. I remember suffocating on the frightening scene I'd left behind.

3

Trauma

O f my brothers and me, I was the one most prone to getting hurt. My knees and elbows were always scraped and scabbed from playing outdoors. I recall two traumatic childhood ordeals in particular.

"Paul, Paaaul!" Mom hollered to Dad. "Come quickly!"

Warm blood ran down my cheek and dripped onto my shirt. I'd been watching Saturday morning cartoons in the playroom with my brothers and had reached down from the daybed to pet Sam, our newly acquired mutt. Being a bit fidgety and startled by touch, Sam promptly leapt up and bit me just below my right eye. Mom ran to grab a hand towel.

"Paul!" she shouted again.

At age five, a little blood didn't startle me, but Sam's reaction did. My body shuddered as Mom touched the towel to my face.

Luckily, Dad was home that day. Running into the playroom, he placed a wad of gauze and pressure on my cheek, and whisked me into the car and to the hospital where he worked as a surgeon. There a pleasant nurse spoke to me in a calm voice as

Dad took care of my face, carefully numbing my cheek and sewing stitches across it.

"I'm gonna get some honeysuckle!" my brother Paul shouted as he raced across the kitchen. At age six, I was determined to follow my older brother everywhere. He pushed open the door and disappeared outdoors. As I ran and straightened my arm to catch the door, it swung back, and the speed of my body caused my right arm to shatter the door's glass. My wrist was sliced open and bled terribly, and several smaller cuts up my arm wept red.

Fortunately, Dad was home and sped me to the hospital. Again, the kindness and nurturing of the hospital staff made me feel safe. At home my parents helped me manage with one usable arm, and made sure I kept the stitches and bandages out of the pool and bathtub. Mom rubbed cocoa butter on the scars daily to keep the tissue soft and help it heal.

These experiences gave me an appreciation for able and compassionate caretakers, for nurturing parents, and for a body that miraculously navigated toward health. I learned that medical personnel were kind and efficient, that my parents had wisdom to guide the process of healing, and that with practical care my body would get what it needed to mend.

In the hospital emergency room after the rape, a nurse sat with me to take my vitals. The fluorescent lights, excessively bright, increased my sense of vulnerability.

"Is there a friend or family member we might contact for you?" she inquired.

"Yes, I'd like my friend Ted to know I'm here." I gave her his phone number.

I was promptly taken into the examining room, where the nurse explained the procedure of gathering evidence for a rape kit. She told me the rape kit is a data collection protocol to gather and preserve physical evidence following sexual assault allegations. It was, of course, my choice if I wanted to cooperate with the police and provide this evidence. Yes, I would cooperate.

Meanwhile, a hospital volunteer had entered the room. She was short and stout, wearing a green polyester blouse buttoned to the neck, a paisley skirt that extended to her shins, and black pumps. With starched hair and red lipstick, and a small worn Bible in hand, she looked like she'd just come from church.

"I'm happy to pray for you," she said without introduction. "You know you can be forgiven for your sins."

I felt steam rise within me. I glanced her way and in a stern voice said, "I'd like you to leave." I wouldn't have anyone placing judgment on me for something that was clearly not my doing.

The nurse examined my face and mouth and determined that stitches were in order, but they would have to wait until after the rape kit was complete. When the doctor arrived, he began his examination and evidence gathering. He spoke about cycling and topics other than what was obviously at hand while he swabbed and poked inside of me, combed through my pubic hair, and collected samples from my mouth. The nurse took my favorite blue biking shorts and bloodstained shirt, packed them in a brown paper bag, and added them to the evidence.

There was nothing that felt gentle about the exam except, perhaps, the doctor's voice, which drifted like waves—in and out—as the rip tide of my body's shock kept pulling me under. I heard what seemed essential: "You'll need a day-after pill to prevent pregnancy. And it's best to follow up with a pregnancy test just to make sure . . . this can be done at the clinic next door . . . you'll need to be tested for HIV . . . this has to happen six months from now . . ." Strangers in hospital scrubs and their words spun in and out of my awareness until I wasn't quite certain this was really happening to me.

Meanwhile, the doctor stitched my gaping lip and examined my mouth, where my two front teeth hung loosely from swollen gums. "You'll need to see a dentist, preferably today. These two teeth may not make it." The exam complete, I was guided to a nearby room, still dressed in a thin green paper hospital gown.

The police arrived to collect the bagged evidence and to ask a myriad of questions. Two male officers stood, one on either side of me, as I reclined on the hospital bed in a room that felt exceptionally small. The nurse walked in, phone in hand. She nudged her way next to me.

"Ted is on the phone for you."

My eyes began to tear as I took the phone. The policemen stepped to the edge of the room and waited as I spoke with my friend.

"Hey, girl, what's going on?" Ted's voice was gentle.

"I was raped." I choked on the words, still in disbelief. It was the first time I spoke the phrase; it wouldn't be the last.

"I'm leaving work now. I'll get there as soon as I can," he said.

I felt relieved—and angry. Relieved, of course, because a friend was coming to help; angry because our meeting wouldn't be infused with the joy and laughter that was typical of our time together.

The police continued their interrogation, doing their best to gather details, most of which I couldn't provide. "Can you tell me what happened . . . after the act of making love?" one officer asked. I was dumbfounded by his gross insensitivity, and speechless. I drifted away again, unable to answer his question.

It was a relief to see Ted walk in the door. The nurse and detectives talked among themselves for a short while after he arrived, then turned to me. The officers were eager to have me show them where the crime had occurred. Returning to that spot was the last thing I wanted, but too agitated to object and wanting to put the whole experience behind me, I agreed and asked Ted to meet me later at my apartment. My cycling clothes had been taken as evidence, so I had no proper clothing and was promptly loaded into a squad car still in my paper gown and wearing no underwear. I was shuttled by the detective and two male officers out of town and northward to where, just two hours prior, I'd been happily pursuing a destination that was now blurred with horrors I couldn't begin to process.

Detective Wentz, the officer in charge, asked me to lead them, and we tromped through the woods to the spot where the crime had occurred. I held the edges of the paper gown close to my thighs to prevent additional exposure. Sure enough, my bike helmet lay abandoned amidst the composted leaves. My red Trek 400 was retrieved from the side of the road, then covered in black fingerprint dust and placed in the back of the squad car.

From the crime scene, Detective Wentz delivered me and my bicycle directly to my apartment. I felt confused and disoriented, my face blue and swollen, my teeth still hanging by threads . . . *that would require attention today.* Wentz stood in the open door of my apartment, explaining what would need to take place next from his perspective.

"Can you come by the station tomorrow morning? With your help, we can begin the process of identifying the perpetrator."

I agreed. They would begin more in-depth investigation to see if anyone in the area had seen the man or his car.

"Is there a friend who can stay with you the next few days?" he asked.

I had lived in the area for only a year, and though I'd made friends, this request seemed rather intimate. I decided to call

Lisa, a math teacher who lived just down the road. She invited me to stay with her.

As Wentz was preparing to leave, Ted called; he would be at my apartment soon. I was relieved to know he was on his way. I showered, scrubbing furiously to erase the morning's atrocities. When Ted arrived, I hugged him and smiled. Still, our connection felt stilted, my bruised, swollen, stitched face and mouth wedged between us. I desperately longed to feel normal again.

"I'm so sorry for you, Anne," he said.

"If I hadn't been trying to avoid that 'Oh Nelly' hill, this probably wouldn't have happened," I joked.

This drew laughter, though it didn't hold the carefree, fun-loving feeling I cherished between us.

"What can I do to help?" Ted was earnest.

"The doctor said my teeth should be treated today. I don't have a dentist in Manassas yet. Do you know anyone I could see?"

Ted began calling dentists and found one who could see me that day. Outside of the calls, neither of us talked much, and the words we couldn't say felt deafening.

I tried to busy myself—preparing a bag to stay the night at Lisa's, wiping the already clean kitchen counter. Any idle moments left me frozen in time, hearing the rapist's voice and feeling myself forced into submission. My body, heavy with the lurid facts of the day, shuddered, and my insides began to feel icy and numb. I did my best to focus on the kindness of Ted, my close yet somewhat new friend who had left work early to support me, but it was hard.

By then it was mid-afternoon, and I wanted to do something mindless—anything to escape the heaviness I felt. Greg had shown up to see how he could help, and the three of us went to the movies. At the concession counter, we got a cup of ice that

I held against my mouth as I sat in the darkness with my comrades and watched *Terminator 2*. I barely remember the film. Its chain of dramatic action scenes seemed to pale in light of what I'd just experienced, but I felt comforted to be in the presence of friends and doing something that felt normal.

Dr. Dollard, the dental surgeon, had kindly agreed to work me in after office hours that day, and at five o'clock Greg drove me to his office. I learned the roots of two of my front teeth had been damaged. The dentist cemented them to neighboring teeth with a white rib of plaster that clouded my smile. We would wait, he said, to see if the roots were strong enough to survive the impact. If not, root canals were the solution.

Somehow I got to Lisa's apartment, and I slept in bed with her. Strange as that was, not knowing her well, I felt grateful I wasn't alone. In the middle of the night, sleepless, I visited the bathroom and was shocked by what I saw in the mirror. My mouth was grossly disfigured by stitches and cemented teeth. With the bruising and swelling, I didn't look at all like myself. I stood in a stupor, staring at my reflection. *Dear God, what's happened to me?* It wasn't just my face that had been disfigured; my whole being felt wrenched out of alignment. I'd been damaged far beyond the bruises and cuts of my childhood. My wounds felt deep, inhumane. Again, I felt myself floating somewhere outside my physical experience, unsure about moving forward, fearful that at any moment I could be terrorized, and unable to discern where or how I could feel safe.

4

Certainty

As a young girl, I'd never feared for my safety. I felt cared for by my family and safe in our small town. I was fortunate to enjoy a childhood filled with the freedom to explore whatever I was curious about. Looking back, I can see that though safety wasn't an issue, I did seek certainty.

My ten-year-old mind loved brainteasers and logic puzzles. When Scholastic Book Club order forms showed up in my school cubby, I'd promptly circle the problem-solving books as my top purchases. New books in hand, I'd plow through each challenge and check my answers in the back for accuracy.

In grade school, I was skilled at math and liked predictable patterns. I loved identifying the unknown in an equation, arriving at the perfect answer, and circling it on my paper. I noticed that certain behaviors produced reliable results. For example, taking lots of notes and memorizing all the facts, rather than just a few, produced a better test grade. Speaking up in class caused teachers to like you. Arranging Mom's numerous magazines in a neat stack on the coffee table made the house feel ordered and more comfortable.

Certainty

At the beginning of my sophomore year in high school, my family moved from Barnesville, Ohio, to Oxford, North Carolina. It wasn't a move I favored; I wanted to stay near my childhood friends, my grandma, and a town I knew well. But my parents had lived in Barnesville for nearly twelve years, and Dad was raised there. They'd been wanting to make a fresh start in a community that was new to both of them and were excited about this next chapter in their lives.

Once settled into Oxford, I missed the familiar places and people of my hometown. At the Methodist church, I missed sitting beside my grandma—Dad's mom—as I'd done every Sunday in Ohio since I was a child. I missed my warm connection to people in the congregation; the pianist at Barnesville Methodist had been my weekly piano teacher, her brother my dentist. I'd known where families sat and could eye my best friend two aisles away. In Oxford there were no familiar faces. I found myself searching for some undefined grounding cord to grasp onto, to make things feel more certain in my new environment. Though I didn't find this in the church service, Sunday school connected me with a kind and welcoming group of teens and with Mr. J, our Sunday school teacher.

Mr. J was in his mid-thirties, young at heart and popular with teenagers. He was wise and introspective and encouraged us to talk about challenging topics. He took the time to learn who I was and devoted an occasional evening to visiting with me and my peers in his home, guiding us as we discussed life and our role in it. As I spent more time with Mr J and reflected within my group of peers, I began to feel some inner certainty and a sense of belonging.

I recall my sense of certainty being challenged within weeks of arriving at college. Oberlin, a private liberal arts school in

Ohio, has a rich history of social justice; students are known to stand for something, even if they're standing alone. So it wasn't unusual to be challenged on one's statements or beliefs. I lived in a coed dorm, and one afternoon some fellows from the first floor came visiting. They stood in our dorm room, questioning my roommate and me about where we were from and our families. The conversation turned to religion; I mentioned I was Protestant—Methodist. An upperclassman confronted me.

"If there's a God, you should be able to prove it," he said. His tone was smug.

Proof was something I knew well from years of problem-solving, but this was a problem I couldn't calculate. It had too many variables. For days, I felt the harshness of the upperclassman's voice and pondered how I might prove my beliefs, but I wasn't even sure how to begin. God was a concept I'd adopted from church, not one I'd established from my own experience. I journaled my thoughts, trying to identify something I could claim with certainty, but I came up empty and soon felt frustrated. My foundation began to rock. I wrote letters to Mr. J, petitioning him with questions: "How can I substantiate belief in a God? How can I worship a God I don't know exists?" On holiday breaks, I scheduled time with Mr. J to sit and engage in philosophical conversations about life and faith. This problem needed to be solved; its solution, for me, could be life changing.

It was this inability to provide proof of my belief that further inspired my interest in mystery and the unknown. I occasionally attended church services while in college, but doing so didn't help me define what I believed. This lack of certainty fueled my curiosity, and I continued my search by taking religion classes and learning about the history of religion and of the God I claimed to worship.

Certainty

At the same time, Dad wanted me to pursue *worthwhile* studies, not soft sciences like psychology or sociology, which he viewed not only as unsubstantiated sciences but also as spotted with quackery and fluff. So I steered clear of both subjects and studied chemistry; it offered the satisfaction of reliable patterns and predictable answers yet still held considerable mystery. I loved working simultaneously with the seen and the unseen.

My religious studies were equally satisfying, revealing patterns in doctrines and practices of world religions and highlighting humankind's powerful desire for meaning. Perhaps discovering my own spiritual truth was more important than proving the existence of God. Though I liked the certainty of proof, I was inspired by exploring the mystery and intrigued with the pursuit of self-knowledge.

In my junior year, I was invited to pursue honors research in chemistry for my final year of college. The commitment felt daunting—hours of study in the laboratory, writing an honors thesis with presentation to the faculty. I was much more interested in studying religion.

"You're gonna accept the honors invitation, aren't you?" Dad asked presumptuously one evening on the phone.

"I'm really enjoying religion classes," I said. "My religious studies professor feels I could complete my minor and perhaps pursue a double major."

"What would you do with a religion major?" I felt Dad was not expecting an answer so much as making a point. At some level I knew he was simply watching out for my future, pushing me toward a pragmatic choice that could lead to greater possibilities down the road.

I had no response. I didn't know what I'd do with it. I only knew I enjoyed studying the mystery, the pursuit of answers that weren't yet certain to me. At that time, I wasn't one to push back, so I chose honors chemistry research. Perhaps Dad was right; it was more practical, and more certain. I wasn't ready to stray too far outside certainty.

The countless details that require attention in the aftermath of assault are likely, for many, a nightmare, and I did my best to maintain business as usual. Since I was on summer break from teaching at the time, my days were not filled with the numerous activities that teaching demanded. Without these familiar demands, however, time felt jumbled and chaotic. I was challenged to find tasks that gave me a sense of predictability and certainty. I focused on keeping my records in good order. I filed medical bills first with the health insurance company, then refiled them with the state's victim compensation plan. I made numerous to-do lists: follow-up calls to assure the state was covering all my expenses, that law enforcement was doing all it could to identify the perpetrator, and that I was scheduling necessary appointments with health professionals.

This ordering and reordering, making calls and putting things in their perfect place, kept me sane the first few weeks after the rape. Once school began, there were teaching responsibilities as well—creating lesson plans, designing and preparing labs, grading papers—all of which satisfied my affinity for checking things off a list and maintaining some sense of control over matters. I craved the certainty that something—anything—in my life could feel whole and complete.

Outside of my daily tasks, fear consumed me. I abandoned my search to understand life and my place in it; there was enough to deal with emotionally. At times it was all I could do to pull myself out of the safety of my apartment and face the onslaught of daily moments of panic that obstructed my clear thinking as well as my ability to breathe comfortably.

Certainty

Though I did everything in my power to keep the chaos at arm's length while I focused on tasks that produced a semblance of normalcy, my body was in a continuous state of hyper-alert and seemed to be operating independently of my mind and intentions. As much as I'd will my body to behave—to slow my breathing, relax my shoulders, stop peering nervously behind me—I could not convince my body and mind to turn off the red flashing lights and blazing sirens. These alerts repeatedly reminded me I was not safe. At least that felt certain.

5

Family

T he thought of delivering news of my traumatic plight to my family felt uncomfortable and distressing. I wasn't sure how to do it, or when. Early in the morning the day after the assault, I met with Detective Wentz at the police station to gather more information about the crime. Later that morning, my cycling friend Dave arrived from Newport News, Virginia. I'd called him the night before. He took off work and drove up first thing in the morning to be with me.

Dave and I had met the previous summer on a Bike Virginia ride, a six-day bicycle tour across the state that wove through tiny mountain communities and beautiful rolling hills. The day I arrived for the tour, Dave was seated in a rocking chair on the porch of a historic hotel in Natural Bridge, Virginia. As I went to check in, he exchanged a "howdy" with my "hello." Dave was good-humored, refreshingly spirited, and easy to be with. With bright red hair receding from his brow, he was easy to recognize in crowds of cyclists at rest stops. Attracted to his kind blue eyes and mischievous smile, I quickly befriended him. After the tour we continued to see one another, traveling back and forth between Manassas and Newport News on weekends, cycling and visiting. Our relationship deepened, and we became more intimate. We had met one another's families and taken some car trips together, traveling to Hawk Mountain in Pennsylvania to watch raptors migrate, and within Virginia to hike parts of the Appalachian Trail.

Dave was observant and sensitive and understood me in a way that most people didn't. Though I thoroughly enjoyed our time together, I had decided I wasn't ready for a steady relationship and had shared those feelings with Dave just a month earlier in the summer of 1990. We remained friends.

I was immensely relieved to see Dave the morning after the rape; his presence helped me feel grounded and reminded me who I was amidst the turmoil I felt inside. Though normally very independent, I felt I needed to lean, to have a levelheaded ally help me make decisions. Dave was sturdy and practical, and I trusted him.

"You're gonna need your family's support," he encouraged. "How 'bout I drive you through to see your folks?"

"I'm not ready for that, Dave. I want to get through this on my own. My dad will be devastated."

I was less concerned about Mom. She was the anchor of our family, always steady, positive and supportive. Dad, on the other hand, was more emotional. His response would be instinctive and unpredictable, and I could already feel myself becoming unhinged by the potential interaction.

Despite my resistance, Dave had soon orchestrated my packed bag, loaded me in his aging white-and-yellow Bronco, and was driving me south. Most of the trip, I sat in silence, hugging my body and not wanting to converse. I didn't need to talk about what had happened to me, though I knew Dave would be open to it. I felt distant and raw.

A Fierce Belief in Miracles

As we rode along, I thought of a simpler time, recalling details from childhood when it felt easy to be with my parents. In my mind the kitchen smelled of fresh-baked bread and coffee; Mom stood at the sink eyeing a titmouse at the feeder; her jeans, dirtied and worn at the knees, celebrated a morning of gardening. Dad, in shorts and a dingy T-shirt, sat at the head of the kitchen table—his ready-for-lunch spot. He was reading the *Christian Science Monitor*, which he held folded in his left hand. His right arm motioned unconsciously back and forth in the air, casting an imaginary fly rod. On the table was his beer stein, chilled and brimming with a golden froth from the basement tap. I imagined curling up on the daybed in my parents' family room, pulling the plaid woolen blanket around my legs, and hiding away there for as long as I needed.

The further south we traveled, the more fidgety I became. The aged Bronco jostled us even on smooth interstate roadway. "I need to get these wheels balanced," Dave said with a chuckle. "This old beast shakes like a dog who ate a handful of tacks." Such analogies were Dave's style—a simple humor that kept me connected to him, and in that moment it provided a lightness that miraculously coexisted with my despair.

Shortly before reaching the North Carolina border, I asked if we could stop. Dave pulled out at a rest area. We walked around the grassy lawn. It was drizzly, and the dampness made the summer heat feel heavy.

I plopped down atop a picnic table, the moisture of the wood penetrating my shorts. "I don't think I can go through with this, Dave," I said, tears suddenly overflowing to my cheeks. I was embarrassed by how unsteady I felt. *Why can't I pull myself together?*

Dave comforted me in a gentle way.

"Regardless of how they react, your folks want to support

you. It's better for them to learn about this now than later." He paused. "You're not worried about them rejecting you in any way, are you?"

"No. But I don't want them to be hurt. I don't want them to see me like this." I couldn't hide my face. I couldn't hide the bruises, the stitches, the cemented teeth.

I had called that morning and spoken with Mom. I told her Dave and I were driving down for the day. I didn't volunteer any more information. She was surprised but didn't inquire further. She promised to have lunch ready for us.

Mom was working in the yard when we pulled into the driveway; she looked up and smiled. My stomach felt heavy. Dave stepped out of the driver's seat and offered a "howdy" and a hug to Mom. I climbed out of the Bronco, keeping my distance to delay Mom's seeing my swollen face.

Walking around the front of the car, I offered, "Hi, Mom," with forced enthusiasm. Her cheery demeanor evaporated when our eyes met.

"What happened to you?"

My eyes shifted to Dave, and he nodded supportively.

"I was out riding my bike, and . . ." Tears welled in my eyes as I fought them back. *Perhaps I should make up another story— something innocent, less traumatic. I don't want Mom to ache for me . . . but then, it's probably best to get this out as quickly as possible.*

"I was raped, Mom."

"Oh, Anne," Mom gasped as she, too, broke into tears. There was nothing any of us could say at that point to clear the air, so we were silent as Dave and I followed her into the house. Dad met us in the kitchen, and I shared the news with him.

He seemed unable to focus on the conversation and fumbled with his words as he sought to respond. He chose to focus on the professionals who'd treated me.

"Who was the emergency doctor? The dentist? What were their names?"

I felt hurt that Dad couldn't ask how I was doing or if I was okay. *This is simply what he needs to know, the first point of focus for him*, I reasoned. In retrospect, it was more than that. The intense emotion was difficult for all of us, especially for Dad, who was good at taking needed action steps to remedy a problem. I later learned that he wrote personal notes of gratitude to the doctor and dentist for taking good care of me.

We ate lunch without much conversation. Dave understood the need for us to have family time and didn't stay long. When my parents agreed to return me to Manassas, he gave me a hug and went on his way.

I'd grown up in a family that shared enriching conversation, dry straight-mouthed humor, and lots of silence. Grief was processed alone, tears shared with pillows. I wasn't practiced in dealing with big emotion, especially in the presence of my parents. When we moved from Ohio to North Carolina and I missed my friends, my hometown, my grandma, I didn't share much of my sorrow and disappointment with my parents. I knew nothing could be done about it, so it seemed more practical to keep my feelings private. It's not that my parents didn't care, but our family focused attention on what was sensible and productive; tears didn't rank high in this category.

I stayed with my parents for only a couple days, sleeping soundly in the safety of my childhood home and a familiar bed. But I needed to return to my apartment; teachers were due back at school soon, and before students arrived I had things to pull together, not least of which was myself.

That fall and winter, Dad encouraged me to put the rape behind me, pull up my bootstraps, put a smile on my face, and continue on. It was, of course, the advice of someone who pushed away his own emotions. But as much as I tried, I couldn't just pack it away. The fear, the anxiety, the breathlessness, the jitters, the anger kept rising up in me in ways that felt completely out of control. I felt disabled by the stress, and it didn't help to know Dad expected me to keep on the sunny side. I would pull up my straps only to find they weren't attached to boots, and so I stood there, feeling naked and helpless.

Mom, on the other hand, didn't discuss the rape unless I brought it up. She had a good sense of how to steady life, how to bring focus back to experiences that were grounding—like providing the next homemade meal, having a needle and thread handy for what needed mending —simple acts that were comforting and kept life moving forward gently one step at a time. Though I wouldn't be able to lean much on Mom with my grief and anger, her presence was nurturing. But in my new Manassas home, I'd need to find other sources of support.

I understood that my parents had a difficult time processing the emotions of this event. They wanted to put it behind them as much as I did, to find a place of comfort and contentment. But comfort and contentment seemed part of a distant past and continued to elude me. I suspected that after that weekend, comfort would continue to elude them as well.

6

Determination

Whitten I met with Detective Wentz at the police department the day after the assault, we had rehashed details of the crime and descriptions of the perpetrator. Prince William County's criminal investigations unit had an antiquated identification process. The ID kit was housed in a metal box with rusted corners and a clasp that was slightly askew. It opened to reveal several compartments, each housing thin sheaths of plastic with various options for facial features. Encouraged by Wentz, I muddled through the images of noses and eyes, laying them out on white paper to see them clearly. The process was absurd; I could draw a better picture of the perpetrator from what I saw in my nightmares. So I did. I then demanded we use a more sophisticated path of identifying the criminal and getting him behind bars. If the county didn't have that capability, I would find someone who did. The task gave me something to focus on, a course I could follow stepwise to reach a specific destination—identifying the perpetrator.

Wentz was accommodating. The next week he drove me to neighboring Fairfax County Courthouse. On the drive he pointed out automobiles in traffic and asked me to look at them to see if I could more exactly identify the make and model of the perpetrator's car.

"That one over there," he'd say, pointing to a Ford Pinto. "Did it look like that?"

If it wasn't red, it didn't register clearly for me. "Yes, something like that," I'd reply.

Once at the courthouse, we stood in a long winding line in the lobby awaiting security clearance to the facility. We shared mundane conversation—education, where we'd lived, hobbies—and avoided talk of cycling or crime. I had my drawing pad with me, which contained multiple sketches of the rapist. I felt eager to get started on creating a solid likeness of the perpetrator and was relieved to finally be admitted to the building where we could focus on the task at hand.

Fairfax County's criminal investigations bureau was modern and efficient. The employee assigned to our case scanned my best sketch and used image-editing software to change colors and features displayed on a large computer screen. I offered my input until the man's face was as close a match as possible to what I could recall. Seeing the rapist's face come into focus was strangely frightening and satisfying at the same time.

The image was shared on major TV networks in DC and surrounding areas, as well as distributed and printed in local newspapers. But there was no response.

Over the next several weeks, Wentz would occasionally drop by my apartment and give me a packet of line-up photos to peruse. Staring at so many faces made them all look the same and muddled my thoughts about what I remembered or didn't remember. Identifying the car was also a problem. I hadn't seen the tags; I only knew the make and color, which wasn't enough to go on. We soon hit a wall, and I was told I would be updated with photos periodically on the chance that one might stand out for me.

Three weeks after the rape, one of my fellow science teachers encouraged me to join her at a self-defense class offered at a community center just down the road from where I lived. Without much consideration, I agreed. The first class was an introduction—some use of voice and simple physical moves. The instructor called us up individually to teach us how to take a positive, grounded stance. After only twenty minutes, I was trembling and tearful. Overwhelmed with emotion, I decided not to return to the class. The experience did little to boost my confidence. Activities where I'd once felt safe and confident, such as walking in a mall, going to the grocery store, or visiting someplace new on my own, such as a doctor's office or a new acquaintance's home, became activities I tended to avoid. I needed to find other ways to assert my power and feel strong again.

Frustrated, I turned to my bicycle. My post-traumatic determination was fierce, and I intended to retrieve not only my passion for cycling but also a life that felt normal. I had a strong bond with my bike, rooted in childhood. At five years old, the training wheels of my first bike had been removed, and with a bit of coaching from Dad, I was whizzing down our driveway on my tiny blue Western Flyer. I remember the wheels responding obediently to my steering, the bike turning in a perfect arc, my body tilting ever so slightly with the frame. Within moments, the bike was a trusted part of me; somehow, it perceived my impulses. Riding it gave me a sense of freedom.

My bike had been my close companion as I navigated my family's move to North Carolina and as I settled into college and then into graduate school. Cycling was where I went when things felt hard to handle and I wanted to be alone. My bike was more than an accessory; it was a trusted guide consistently encouraging my exploration, advocating my self-reliance, holding space for my need to drive hard or coast leisurely. Except for an occasional click of the gears, my bike was a voiceless escort, offering pedals to spin meditatively while I turned thoughts inward. Without the distraction or pressure of conversing with another cyclist, I found solace and connection with a strong inner part of myself. Once employed as a teacher, I had purchased bright blue cycling shorts and a matching jersey. They were my go-to outfit for needed attitude adjustment. Any frustration or sadness and I'd slip on my beloved azure duds, straddle my crimson frame, and coast down the road, allowing the breeze to blow it all behind me.

After the rape, my bicycle sat unused, leaning against my living room wall, spotted with black fingerprint dust. I couldn't bring myself to touch its soiled frame. I felt betrayed. It wasn't the bike's fault; I'd made the choice to go down that gravel road, to push those narrow tires over terrain they'd obviously resisted. Perhaps the bike had tried to tell me, and I just didn't listen. Regardless, our relationship felt muddled and flat.

Once school started, I did my best to use my bike for commuting to work. The school was only five miles from my apartment; I could cycle through pleasant neighborhoods that were safe and helped me avoid much of the rush hour traffic. Sometimes on the ride I identified a whisper of strength within me, but finding something that resembled the joy-filled, carefree Anne I had known just a short time ago felt impossible. It just wasn't in me. Often, just riding would begin a cycle of panic attacks, my breath short and rapid. This would go on for several days or a couple of weeks, my body becoming increasingly anxious—desperate—to drink in a full, life-giving breath. I began to feel angrier and more insistent on riding, just to prove I still could. *The rapist,* I thought, *can take away many things, but he is not going to rob me completely of the serenity I feel on two wheels.*

Unfortunately, he continued to creep incestuously into this precious expression of who I was. Without consistent cycling and the peace and balance it had provided me, I began to feel disempowered, weak, and helpless.

Not long after the school year began, my friend and school security officer Carter asked if I'd like to ride with him on the weekend. I felt torn; part of me wanted to get out for a longer ride, but another part didn't want to put forth the effort. It was a generous offer of time and companionship, and though I felt more drawn to curl up in the safety of my apartment, I knew it would be good for me to go. Leaning into the fear and numbness would only keep me frozen. If I kept pushing beyond my limiting emotions, I had a better chance of finding the other side, which I imagined was gentle and smooth like bike tires on a freshly paved road. I accepted Carter's offer, and we planned to meet Saturday morning in the parking lot near my apartment.

Physical preparation for a ride—putting on cycling shorts, gloves, and a helmet; pumping tires and filling water bottles—was a healthy distraction. And Carter was always easy and fun to be with. I coasted into the parking lot and greeted him cheerily. I quickly learned, though, that Carter wasn't a seasoned cyclist. His bicycle looked like it had sat unattended in a shed for years. What's more, he had a flat.

I pulled out my patch kit and began the work of mending his tube. Mending a tube was second nature to me and normally wouldn't present a challenge. But Carter's flat was enough to deflate my spirit. It seemed as if the universe was conspiring to take away the one activity I felt held the key to my passion and health. I roughed up the rubber with a file and glued a patch over the puncture. Meanwhile, I focused my inner dialogue on

Determination

convincing myself this was not a big deal; there was no reason to let this minor glitch diminish the energy of our ride.

As I pumped air into the newly patched tube and positioned the tire back on the bike, Carter and I spoke of niceties—all the while avoiding any mention of the eight-hundred-pound rapist sitting beside us. My inner dialogue became more forceful in attempts to obscure this unrelenting presence. *I will ride, damn it. I will ride.*

7

Healing

If someone had told me shortly after my trauma that it might take over twenty years to fully heal from the event, I would have scoffed. At age twenty-six, my concept of healing was that results depended on taking the necessary steps: see the doctor, take the pills, rest, and exercise. As the daughter of a physician, I was familiar and comfortable with the model of Western medicine.

After being raped, breathing and ease became elusive. The trauma of the incident permeated the cells of my being in a way I had no control over. As I returned to the classroom that fall, my days were filled with shortness of breath, unpredictable surges of anxiety, and exhaustion after the simplest tasks. And yet I was determined to somehow defy the reality of my daily experience, and be at peace and happily planning my next chemistry class or cycling adventure. As much as I willed this to happen, it wouldn't unfold that way.

Three months after the incident, I attended my first group counseling meeting for victims of sexual trauma. I had been referred by a friend of a friend. Facilitated by a licensed therapist, the group gave women the opportunity to share their stories. About twenty women of varying ages sat in the room. The wood paneling was dark and the lighting subdued. I don't remember much of what was said except for the woman who sat directly across from me. She was stocky and rough-hewn. Her resentment filled the folded metal chair with such intensity I felt the chair might snap under the stress.

"I've been suffering from this for over fifteen years," she said.

That was all I heard—or needed to. I was in the wrong place, I decided. The prospect of carrying my anger and angst for so long felt dreadful. No, I would heal without the group, and I would do it quickly.

But I found myself suffering, unable to make the dread and nervousness subside. It was my second year teaching chemistry at Osbourn Park High School in Manassas. My classroom was on the third floor in the far back corner. The walk to the faculty bathroom was not a formidable distance, just some fifty feet down the hall and around a corner. Students were given five minutes to change classes, during which time I could simply scoot down the hall and around the bend. After the trauma, however, this was no longer a viable option. Students filled the hallways between classes with movement and talk. I couldn't predict what might happen there, and a simple walk to the restroom induced hampered breathing and severe anxiety.

I tried to focus on things I could control: the curriculum, grading, connecting with individual students as they entered the classroom. But the slightest thing would throw me into uncontrollable angst that could take hours or days to subside.

Out on the town, I was convinced the rapist was nearby, and in the strangest places. My cycling friend Greg and I had decided to go out to eat one Friday evening in October. He drove into Manassas from Arlington and took me east on I-66 to a nice little restaurant. We were sharing a meal and good conversation when the rapist walked up to the bar near our table. He wore a blue baseball cap. I could only see the left side of his face, and with the soft lighting I wasn't sure of his hair color. But I knew it was him—I'd recognize him anywhere. I couldn't take my eyes off him and was soon in a panic. I needed to get out of there, fast. Greg, who was levelheaded and aware of my edginess, took quick action. He flagged the waiter, paid our bill, and guided me out to the safety of his car.

Later that fall, I walked into the apartment management office to pay my monthly bill. It was mid-afternoon, and sun poured in through the skylights and the large bay window behind the receptionist. The clubhouse was quiet, the soft billowy couches filled with colorful pillows. And the man who had raped me stood in the lobby, just a few feet away. Suddenly skylights and windows were clouded, the cheery decor became gray, and my chest felt constricted. The rapist was speaking with someone and had his back to me, but I knew his dirty-blond hair, his rough demeanor. And I could discern the forceful tone in his voice. My heart was racing. My breath stuck in my throat, and I began to choke. I couldn't let him see me.

Without paying my bill, I ran in a panic back to the safety of my apartment, locked the door, curled up on the couch, and began to cry. Once my tears dried, I called home and relayed my fear to my parents. Years later I learned that my parents had called the apartment office that afternoon to encourage action if there was a threatening presence and to ask the staff to somehow keep an eye on me for my safety and well-being.

I knew these feelings and thoughts were not rational, but they haunted me and nothing seemed to clear them. With the memory constantly in awareness, I lived in a hyperalert state.

The stress of the trauma grew worse as weeks passed. I slept poorly, which compounded my anxiety. Knowing how difficult it was for me to get up the strength to face the day, my neighbor Michelle was kind enough to fix tea for me early each morning before I went to school. We would sit at a small parlor table on the edge of her kitchen with warm mugs and try to keep the conversation light and infused with laughter.

Michelle was my age and had experienced multiple violent assaults. While my emotional terrain felt untamed, she seemed to contain her feelings well. I likely had some things to learn from her, but I didn't have the capacity to take them in at the time. It was enough to get out the door each morning, and I was grateful for our daily connection that grounded me to do just that.

For Christmas that year, my parents gave me a puppy, in hopes that a companion would give me a sense of safety. Chelsea was a Brittany, covered with caramel spots and freckles; she was chunky and playful. She loved running and jumping and chewing on anything in sight. Unfortunately, Chelsea had to be left gated in my tiny kitchen during the day. The neighbors could hear her barking, which was stressful for me to think about during the school day. I worried that I wasn't caring for her as best I could and soon had a neighbor stop by daily and take her out to walk during the day.

When I arrived home, Chelsea was always desperate for attention and ready for an extended walk in the Manassas Battlefields down the road. But the walk wasn't enough exercise for her, and she was unsettled at night, depriving me of rest and making me even more jittery during the day.

As Chelsea grew, she was soon able to clear the fence at the entrance to the kitchen and made a hobby of ravaging my houseplants, splattering potting soil across the beige carpet. Many days I returned from school to face an evening of cleaning house and taking inventory of what needed to be moved higher or hidden to avoid the puppy's curious mouth. Though these chores offered tasks I could focus on and accomplish, they quickly became too much.

In January of 1991 it was time to get my six-month HIV test as a follow-up from the rape. I made an appointment at the clinic and met with a nurse who drew blood to send to the lab. I was told I'd need to wait two weeks for the results. That same week, our country declared war with Iraq. Given my imbalance, I resonated with the heightened emotions related to war, especially living just outside the nation's capital. My breathing became so shallow that on most days I felt dizzy and disoriented. With afternoons spent cleaning up after the puppy, preparing for the next day's lesson, then spending a fretful night in bed, I was exhausted on many levels.

It was midday on a Tuesday. I was standing by the ebony lab bench lecturing to students and felt myself fading. I held onto the desk, its smooth black surface cool under my fingertips. There was an equation on the wipe board at the front of class that I was intending to refer to . . . something else I needed to say . . . and then everything became dark and quiet. I remember waking at my friend Stella's home, a soft pillow beneath my head, sunlight filtering through her sheer curtains, her voice whispering to me. Healing—I desperately needed healing.

As much as I loved the liveliness and laughter-inducing antics of my puppy, I also knew she needed to go. The first chance I had to get away for a weekend, I drove to my parents' home and delivered Chelsea back to them. There she would live, hunt, and run for the next twelve years. She was well cared for. I needed to care for me.

A fellow teacher referred me to a psychotherapist in Reston,

Healing

Virginia, and I scheduled an appointment. Her office was in a small redbrick building shared with other therapists. The glass door opened into a large rectangular waiting room, sparsely furnished with a few chairs against blank walls and a floor covered with dirty off-white carpet. All the offices situated around the room had brown, unlabeled doors. I waited for the appropriate door to open and reveal the therapist I was to meet. I was not feeling good about our encounter. I had grown up with a father who often spoke disparagingly about those who practiced psychology. This compounded my sense that being emotional—showing grief or anger—exemplified weakness. So before stepping foot in a therapy office, I had established my own ideas about what the appointment symbolized, and my unfavorable judgment heightened my anxiety.

Therapist—I read the word as "the_rapist." And that's what therapy represented to me: a stranger trying to bare my private parts. I didn't like the idea of talking about the rape—the details were repulsive. I preferred to put it behind me and focus on anything else. I cringed at the thought of being seen by a stranger in all my instability and powerlessness. I persisted against the inner voice of anxiety only because I knew I needed help. Given that things were obviously out of control and wearing on me in excessive ways, I could at least attempt counseling.

One of the brown doors opened on the hour, and a middle-aged woman with dark hair and glasses stepped into the lobby and introduced herself. She seemed kind and invited me through her door and into a comfortable wing chair in her office. We spoke casually for a bit; then I asked her something I'd been considering.

"Can I heal through laughter instead of tears?" I thought it a grand idea. Surely a person could laugh their way to happiness and wholeness. I'd learned early in life that the best gift you can give someone is a smile—such a simple thing that we often forget to give. I was a smiley child and received lots of reinforcement for it, so it stuck. I befriended many with my smile and often didn't realize it. So innocent I was, and unaware that my immediate friendliness might one day cause me grief.

"No," the_rapist said. "This is therapy. There will be tears."

But I preferred smiling, and so I did. I believed that appearing happy and keeping tears and anger in check were synonymous with strength. I could just pretend it hadn't happened. *I wasn't really hurt that bad,* I told myself. *But my teeth, my smile* . . . By then I had undergone two root canals, and my front teeth had begun to discolor. I couldn't seem to let go of the thought that he took away my smile.

At the time, I wasn't aware I was avoiding emotion. I couldn't imagine that my anger and grief might be beneficial in achieving the goal of inner peace and balance. So I pushed away the anger and grief, disregarded the tears that bubbled up unexpectedly, and did my best to plow forward despite my difficulty with the moment-to-moment task of breathing.

After a couple months of weekly meetings, the therapist recommended I consider a program called DC IMPACT Self Defense that would be offered to the public that spring. I wasn't sure I was ready, since the self-defense training I'd attempted in August had resulted in tears at the first class. What the therapist described sounded even more foreboding, with padded aggressors who would play-act threatening situations with participants. But I'm not one to wince and retreat. Knowing it could be helpful—if I could get through it—I decided to give it a try.

DC IMPACT was held in the basement of a church in downtown DC. It didn't seem like the safest area of town, but I was able to park nearby before the sun set and felt fine once I settled in with this new group of women. We each shared our experience and intentions for the class. I felt closely bonded after hearing the other women's stories of rape, incest, living with fear. I knew I would be supported and vowed to be present for the other women as best I could.

We met weekly and practiced asserting ourselves with our voice and a set of prescribed physical moves. Then we were introduced to mock assailants who hid behind extensive padding and headgear, their 250-pound bodies offering a threatening presence against which we could practice defending ourselves and feel the confidence we'd gained in facing our fears.

One evening, after the fourth class, I got in the car and noticed my breathing. It was full—filling my lungs and body with sweet life. Somehow during the class I had opened up some part of me, screamed or punched or expressed my anger, and released some of my resistance. It was the first time I noticed that my physical condition and my anger were connected. I wasn't sure how to explain it, but I felt deeply grateful for a reprieve from the constant gasping for breath. This experience gave me hope, and that evening I cried tears of joy.

Some weeks later, our class held a public graduation. I invited my female colleagues from school to witness me at this event. It was an afternoon of heightened emotion—women propelled from their silence into eruptions of "NO! STOP! BITE! DIAL 911!" I was moved by my female warriors, knowing the inside stories they had shared and what it took for them to stand their ground, shout their worthiness, fight for their lives. It was no different for me. As I walked out on the mat, I felt the energy surge within me. Each choice and action, each verbal response and targeted strike, was a sweet release on many levels. I was ready for what lay ahead. I had certainty in my physical ability and trusted I could face my fear.

8

Love

I had no desire to date men after I was raped, and in April of 1991 I declared to my family over spring break that I'd made the decision to remain a single woman.

This was due in large part, of course, to my trauma. But there was also Martie. Just two months after the rape, Martie contacted me and asked if I'd like to get together. We had met several years prior while cycling in northern Virginia; he had since moved to nearby Reston. We hadn't seen each other for almost three years. Remembering the fun we'd had riding together, I agreed to go out with him. I thought that getting in touch with an old friend could be healing. My trauma was still fresh, and because I felt as if its effects were as visible as boils on my skin, I couldn't be with friends and say nothing about it. Rape was at the forefront of my experience. Martie's response to hearing I'd been raped, however, was not only unexpected but almost inconceivable.

"What the hell were you doing riding alone out there?" he exclaimed.

"I have every right to ride those roads," I said. I knew instantly that our date was a bad idea.

Martie insisted on giving me a lesson in self-defense, and I didn't think to ask what experience he had. He drove me to his father's business offices in a large warehouse on the edge of Reston—a place where I could be loud, he explained. My lungs constricted and my stomach tightened at the thought. I had trouble getting oxygen into my system and began to swallow big gulps of air so I wouldn't become light-headed. I felt beyond vulnerable; I was not safe. Tears began to well up in my eyes. I didn't want to be loud, and certainly not in Martie's presence.

Martie was trying to help in the only way he knew how. On some level, I felt I was showing weakness by not wanting to learn new ways to appear strong and confident. *Perhaps I should push through these emotions and learn how to use my voice more effectively. If I can't do this, maybe I'll never get beyond my fear.* But another part of me was clear that my date with Martie was not the time for pushing through fear, and despite my hampered breathing, my voice didn't falter.

"I'm not doing this," I said. "I appreciate your concern, Martie. I'll do this when I'm ready for it. Right now, I'd like to go home."

Martie conceded and drove me back to my apartment. I never saw him again.

I couldn't fault Martie for his behavior; he likely had no experience with trauma and didn't know how uncomfortable his prodding would make me feel. Unfortunately, I was re-traumatized—and by someone I had trusted. This caused me to doubt myself and my judgment even more, and my confidence relating to men and dating plummeted. I didn't fear men, but I was concerned about my ability to discern who could support me in a helpful and appropriate way. I believed that staying independent and single would shield me from men's apparent need to be directive.

Shortly after my declaration of independence to my family, I met Tom, a fellow teacher at Osbourn Park High School. The school was large, with teachers and students sprawled across three floors; it was no wonder it took most of the school year for us to meet.

I'd been told about Tom throughout the year by a fellow science teacher and mutual friend, Jim. Tom taught in the Tech Ed department. He was a cyclist, and Jim thought we would enjoy each other's company. One Friday afternoon as I wheeled my bicycle toward the door to head home, Jim called to me from across the cafeteria and asked me to wait a moment. He rushed down the hall out of sight and returned shortly with Tom, introduced us, and departed.

Tom and I stood in the sparsely lit, deserted cafeteria and talked. His deep-set eyes looked dark, perhaps tired, but his tousled light brown hair and easy laughter brought out the playful boy in him. We talked of cycling and teaching and what had brought us to Manassas. Tom had built his own log cabin by hand and lived in it while he attended college. In addition to biking, he sometimes rode his BMW motorcycle to work. He loved old-time music and was an accomplished banjo player. In what seemed like moments, I felt I knew Tom well; I connected with his innocence, his fun-loving spirit, and his kind heart. Before we parted, Tom gave me his business card. "Renaissance Man," it read. I laughed. Years later, he told me he was relieved I hadn't rolled my eyes.

The day after we met, I began my training as a volunteer with our city's newly formed Sexual Assault Victim Advocacy Service (SAVAS). This was something I was inspired to do given the insensitivity of a number of people I'd encountered after the rape. The training was over at noon, and Tom and I planned to ride our bikes together. We met at my apartment, donned our bike shorts, filled water bottles, and headed west where roads were less populated. We spent the afternoon riding and visiting briefly as we stopped to check maps and hydrate. Tom was easy and fun to be with. I didn't feel pressured to be or do anything beyond what felt natural and comfortable, which was refreshing. As I'd been commuting to school by bicycle for most of the school year, my legs were strong. Tom, who didn't ride as often, trailed behind. We later joked about how I dusted him.

I felt amazingly at ease with Tom. Maybe I'd convinced myself I wasn't dating; I had, after all, been clear in my intent to stay single. Or perhaps it was Tom's own comfort with himself without any need to impress or appear dominant. Whatever, his presence put me at ease, and I felt an equal partner in our relationship. This was a new and empowering experience and one I quite enjoyed.

On our second date we met at Chili's for dinner. Over a plate of nachos, I shared with Tom that I'd been raped the previous summer. This wasn't a conversation I'd planned, but Tom had seen a poster on my refrigerator from the DC self-defense course. It was bright and colorful, not something you'd miss—splattered with bold words of defense: NO, BITE, ELBOW, EYES, CALL FOR HELP, DIAL 911. Tom asked me what it meant. I felt no shame in sharing my story. I couldn't hide that I'd been traumatized, nor did I want to. Dealing with the fallout of rape challenged me in unpredictable ways, and I needed friends to be advocates for me when I felt out of sorts.

Tom, who'd been conversational up to that point, paused for a moment, and I assumed he was processing this intimate information. His next question caught me off guard.

"How do you define rape?" he asked gingerly, his head tilting ever so slightly.

Rape—both the definition and the experience—had been

just as new to me the previous year. Not only had I been naive about the possibility of it ever happening to me, but I likely couldn't have defined the word. I shared the definition I'd learned at SAVAS: "Rape is defined as vaginal penetration without consent. From what I've learned, about a third of all women are directly affected by sexual violence."

I was incensed by this statistic and wondered how all those women were coping and keeping their heads above water. But in the conversation with Tom, I kept my emotions in check. I didn't want them to get the better of me.

Later that evening, as Tom and I sat visiting in my living room, he shared his sorrow about my trauma.

"I'm really sad to know this happened to you," he said, unexpectedly shedding a few tears. I wasn't used to this display of emotion from men. His upset seemed like a mirror of what I'd held back in our earlier conversation.

"I had no idea how many women . . ." He paused, clearing his throat. "It's just not right."

I felt a little uncomfortable that my new acquaintance was willing to share so intimately in my experience, to touch into a realm that for the past nine months had felt inescapable and isolating. I appreciated his consideration of my experience and the enormity of the issue, and his connection with it on a deep emotional level.

The following weekend I invited Tom for dinner. I prepared lasagna, fixed a green salad, and baked carrot cake for dessert. Tom arrived with flowers, his banjo, and a small box of music cassettes and books he enjoyed and wanted to share with me. I welcomed his warmth and friendship and couldn't help but feel attracted to him, but I felt unsure about getting too close.

Tom was patient and didn't pressure me. He checked in with me often to ask what I was feeling and to understand what he might do to help me feel comfortable with touch and intimacy. I was sensitive to being pushed or coerced into any action and was unnerved by advances that came from behind me; an unexpected touch or embrace from behind would cause me to gasp and retreat. While I felt confident that Tom was trustworthy and respectful, my body didn't yet have that clarity. I did my best to breathe and stay present as I responded to his touch. Even so, I'd still find myself angry or shaken at times for no apparent reason. Somehow, Tom seemed to take it in stride, offering both concern and support while not taking it personally.

We began spending the bulk of our weekends together, driving into DC to visit museums or heading west to the mountains to hike and camp. We left notes for one another in our faculty mailboxes. Tom used clip art printed on a dot matrix printer to create cards that expressed his appreciation for our time together and comically represented something we had discussed or laughed about. We jokingly left pink detention slips in each other's mailboxes, citing disciplinary actions for our budding romance, the reparation being more time together. More than once we called in sick on the same day and played hooky together. One of those days we visited the National Aquarium in Baltimore; on another we went biking and rock climbing. We laughed lots, which made life feel lighter for me, and gradually my spirit as well as my body began to entrust itself to Tom.

As our relationship deepened, I continued to experience symptoms of post-traumatic stress disorder (PTSD) and pain, and was particularly grateful for the friendship and company of someone who was sensitive and attentive to my needs.

My desire to stay in Manassas was waning, and as the school year came to a close I was certain I wanted to leave behind the grief and upset associated with living there. I needed a change of scenery, and perhaps leaving the area would purge me of some stress from the trauma. Tom was also planning a move, and we searched and discussed together. We considered moving to the same town to give our relationship more opportunity to develop. During that time, I continued to seek ways to enhance my inner strength and rekindle my passion for cycling.

"You ought to do a bike tour this summer," Tom encouraged. "When I graduated from college, I traveled out west and rode my bike from Denver to Missoula."

"I'm not sure I'm ready to take that on," I said. While I felt hesitant, I was also inspired by Tom's enthusiasm and knew that a trip that pushed my limits could help build my confidence.

"Study your options. There are plenty of reliable cycling maps and tours available. You could purchase maps and ride yourself or choose a group ride that looks fun. In a group tour, you'll be advised what to bring and the trip will be completely planned for you."

That sounded more comfortable than going it alone. Riding with a group who loved cycling and still being challenged by the distance would be perfect.

"I could see myself doing this. I'll look into it," I said.

I researched options and chose a three-week ride of nearly nine hundred miles with a loaded touring bike through the Canadian Rockies. This felt grand, confidence building, and, I hoped, healing.

It was a wonderful adventure. I flew west to Missoula, Montana, where the ride began. There were eleven of us from all parts of the country, and the ride was full of wilderness and beauty. I enjoyed the group, though on many days I chose to ride solo. This gave me opportunity to stop often, take in the majestic views, reflect and ground myself, and begin processing the events of the past year in a new way. I also began planning what I wanted to do when I returned home.

Love

Tom and I exchanged multiple letters as I journeyed north into Canada, his cards held at post office locations along our cycling route. We repeatedly affirmed that we longed to be together. We spoke whenever we had the chance, and I became known in our group as the rider who spent hours in phone booths.

While I rode out west, Tom moved to the mountains of North Carolina. He invited me to visit him in Asheville when I returned. I was excited about seeing him again; his support during my trip had been endearing, and I missed him. Once back in Manassas, I packed a bag and headed south for a visit. I planned to spend a few days and decide if I would consider moving there.

Asheville is nestled in a beautiful southern portion of the Appalachian Mountains. The nearby forests are easy to access through an extensive trail system, and the Blue Ridge Parkway offers lovely drives past the city by car or bike. Tom had begun work for a mountain bike company that conducted rides in the forest and on the parkway—mostly for tourists. I met him at his place of work at noon on a Saturday. He was busy cleaning bikes and lubricating their components. As soon as he saw me, he dropped what he was doing and hurried over to give me a hug. Sinking into his arms, I felt as if I'd come home.

Tom left work early that day to picnic with me and to spend the afternoon showing me the area. We ventured into the Pisgah Forest to Cove Creek Falls. Rain had turned the woodlands lush and shiny. We hiked and played in the water, and as the sun was getting low in the sky he invited me to climb a steep rock wall with him. It was slick and challenging, but I made it to the moss-covered top where we sat with a perfect view of the setting sun. It was here that Tom pulled a ring out of his pocket and proposed.

"I know this may seem premature," he began, "but I'd love it if we could spend the rest of our lives together."

I felt my face flush. It wasn't something I expected but was certainly something I would consider. Our intimacy was new, and there were questions about my own well-being and what I would do in this new place—so many unknowns. I accepted the ring, and we agreed our engagement would be a testing period. We understood that if our relationship continued to feel strong, we would plan to marry. I felt warmly satisfied with our conversation and agreement, though admittedly without a plan that held any sense of certainty. A few days later I returned to Manassas, packed my belongings into a moving truck, and relocated to Asheville.

Once in Asheville, I experienced weeks of anxiety and breathlessness sourced from some mysterious place that I couldn't yet identify. This was uncomfortable for me and for Tom. He had a knack for fixing things, but trauma could not be remedied with a drill and duct tape. As I grew accustomed to my new surroundings, my concerns were finding the support I needed to address my increased anxiety and considering whether our relationship would work. In my characteristic manner, I wanted certainty that I was making a wise decision with Tom.

I initially moved in with Tom. He was staying in an unfinished bedroom at a friend's home, which was graced with both fresh country air and mountain moisture, leaving leather goods moldy and natural fibers mildewed, especially those still packed in boxes that were stuffed under Tom's bed and stacked at the edges of his room. I soon felt the need to establish my own community and friendships in Asheville and proceeded to find my own place to live. I began to establish more life balance in this process, making my own friends while also spending time with Tom. There were challenges for each of us in finding employment. We spent hours discussing options and encouraging one another in our respective choices, as we were both intent on finding work that was meaningful to us and to those we served. These adjustments required patience and understanding and encouraged us to communicate our needs and feelings with each other.

Fun-loving and adventurous, Tom was always planning something new for us to do; this I loved. Not only was he great at choosing and planning weekend outings, but he went the extra mile to ensure I was comfortable and happy.

"Hey, we oughta ride our bikes across North Carolina," he suggested one spring morning over cantaloupe and muffins.

"Awesome. Let's do it!"

"We could ride from here to your parents' home easily, only about three hundred miles by bike," Tom said. "I've already picked up some cycling maps, and we can carry our tent and gear."

Tom often presented such enticing plans having taken the initial steps to make them happen. He was organized for adventure and kept large plastic crates designated for camping and cycling tours and filled with the essentials. This made the start of an epic journey as simple as packing the camping crate in the car or emptying a cycling crate and loading its contents onto our bikes.

Several weeks later, we drove two cars to my parents' home in Oxford and left one for our return drive. Days later, we had a friend drop us off with our bikes just east of Mount Mitchell— the highest peak on the east coast—to begin our ride. From there we cycled across the central part of the state to my parents' home, some three hundred miles by bike. We camped four nights and rode fifty to seventy miles a day. The trip inspired laughter and stories and fostered closer connection between us. I loved being outdoors and especially spinning wheels with someone whose company I enjoyed. Tom was a man after my heart.

If I was seeking harmony and balance in my life in these early years of our relationship—and I was, on the surface—it didn't appear Tom could offer it. His job with the mountain bike company was part-time for the summer, and he didn't have work lined up for the fall. He was still living out of boxes in his friend's spare bedroom, with no plans to get a place of his own. Tom seemed more interested in playing banjo with the old-time music community and planning the next fun adventure than he did in settling down and creating a secure home. These things were troubling to me. They were also the perfect mirror of my own mixed emotions and competing needs.

What attracted me, however, was the goodness Tom exhibited—always offering a hand, helping to fix things, being a good friend. He also was—and continues to be—a creative thinker, tinkering with things until he finds a solution that works. I didn't know at the time that these qualities helped keep me flexible and open to possibility on my path to healing. Many years later, I could clearly see how much I needed Tom's strong presence to pull me out of my logical mind, to release my need for certainty, to encourage a creative and trusting and more playful approach to life. Tom was the perfect influence and partner.

It would be over two years before our trial period brought us certainty that we were meant for one another and wanted to marry. It was time well worth investing, as we had been through ups and downs and had come to know each other well. We felt confident our relationship would last far into the future.

9

Disclosure

Shortly after settling in Asheville, I contacted *America's Most Wanted,* a television program that highlighted crimes from across the nation with the intent to identify and apprehend criminals. The producers gladly interviewed me and aired a segment about my experience, including the photos created from my drawings and the Fairfax County Police Department's graphics assistance. While I felt some sense of accomplishment, the show produced no findings. Though I didn't want others to suffer at the hands of the man who was still at large if I could prevent it, such fruitless attempts provided little inspiration for me to continue. While my determination to find him faded with time, my pain and angst did not.

The trauma affected me in ways that were unpredictable and sometimes out of control. When my angst reached a threshold, I'd dial the help line at the local rape crisis center and someone would talk me through the chaos. For the most part, I was able to keep my afflictions hidden from other people. The gasping for breath was something I could do silently, and my physical pain was not apparent to others. This was important to me. I was intent on maintaining an appearance of stability and balance. If I could accomplish that, I could almost convince myself everything was okay.

The first couple of years in Asheville I worked as an office manager for a small nonprofit agency. Outside of work, I became a volunteer advocate for the rape crisis center, supporting women in the emergency room after an assault, and taking late-night phone calls from individuals experiencing panic or post-traumatic stress. I was intent on being a solid presence for women who'd experienced sexual violence. I could certainly have benefited from such support when I'd had evidence collected for my own rape kit, and in my interactions with law enforcement.

In the fall of 1994, I began teaching chemistry at a county high school. I enjoyed being in the classroom again; however, I found it troubling to stand in front of a class of teen girls, knowing many of them would be, or already had been, victims of violence. The thought unnerved me. I saw myself in their innocence and naivete and wanted to do something to help them avoid an experience like mine.

My first step toward this goal was to become trained as a member of the rape crisis center speaker's bureau. This gave me the opportunity to speak to young people about boundaries, safe space, and wise choices. It also inspired me to develop my own assertiveness training and self-defense classes. I offered the first of my classes to teen girls after school and was soon teaching multiple programs to groups throughout the county.

The more I presented, the more passionate I became. After two years of teaching chemistry, I quit my job and devoted myself full-time to presenting assertiveness training to groups of girls and women across Western North Carolina. I researched and gathered data so I could offer clear and concise information, practical tools and knowledge about staying safe, and activities that emboldened women to use their voices and bodies to set boundaries and tap into their innate power.

My intent in the trainings was to steer clear of conversations that invoked fear and to focus solely on empowerment. Allowing too much emotion to enter into the equation would have invited uncertainty. For this reason, I didn't share my personal story during the trainings; doing so felt risky and permeated with fear. I wasn't certain how others might react, and I knew their reactions could fuel my own unsteady emotions.

Regardless of the strong presence I appeared to present in facilitating the trainings, I was painfully aware that each participant was providing a mirror of my experience and emotional geography. I was surrounded by fear and angst; it was evident in the women's quiet, hesitant voices and limp body postures as they role-played a threatening scenario. They openly expressed fear of walking alone and living alone. I was angry that so many women carried their fear as a partner through life. Their determination to live free of that fear inspired me to stand taller, speak my mind, and set firm boundaries. I wanted to be a strong role model for them and knew I needed to practice those very things.

The women's fears provoked my own inner beast. My wounds were deep—sometimes feeling hidden and inaccessible—and exacerbated by stress, particularly when I facilitated workshops. My left hip had begun to occasionally "lock" as I walked—a surprising and painful sensation often accompanied by a gasp. This required me to stop, sometimes readjust the angle of my hip joint, and relax a moment before taking a slow step forward.

Not quite a year after the rape, I had begun to experience pain in my pelvis and hips. The pain persisted even after multiple chiropractic treatments. I knew something wasn't quite right, but I continued with activities that seemed to build my confidence. These included facilitating workshops and riding my bike. The workshops were inspirational, and the cycling had begun to give me a hint of my inner strength, a sense of my own power. I needed these pursuits to keep my head above the turbulent waters of post-traumatic stress. To succumb to my physical discomfort was an act I equated with giving in, once again, to the rapist.

I sensed that the emotional pain from my trauma was crying out louder as time passed, and my hip pain grew more pronounced and problematic. Even so, I continued to address only my physical symptoms, delaying a look at the underlying emotion that seemed remote and frightening. I met with multiple alternative health practitioners whom I felt could purge me of the pain and weakness that resided in my hips and restore the expansive breath I'd once experienced.

Meanwhile, strong and self-assured were traits I desperately tried to attain. I observed my thought pattern with frustration: *Perhaps if I had had a stronger presence, a more assertive demeanor, this would never have happened to me. Perhaps if I had looked stronger, that man would have avoided me.* I believed that increasing my self-reliance and inner strength would lessen my fear, so I chose to hide anything that hinted of weakness. Weakness would not keep me safe.

About nine months into my assertiveness work, I was facilitating a training for students at Warren Wilson College. The women were bright, engaged, and inquisitive. I had just shared the introductory material with the class.

"Our local rape crisis center reported 342 rape or attempted rape cases in our county last year. The national statistics tell us that a third of all women are directly affected by sexual violence, and one in five women will be raped in her lifetime. Unfortunately, many rapes go unreported—for multiple reasons—so these statistics are likely quite a bit higher. Now, I understand that hearing these statistics can easily invoke fear, but take heart. Fear and empowerment are two sides of the same coin. I'll be sharing with you some studies that will help you see that learning and practicing simple skills and techniques—which we'll do in this class—will deliver you to a place of greater empowerment, a place where you're much less likely to be targeted for violence and will know what to do if you are."

A young woman raised her hand. She had short blond hair and a pierced nose and was spunky and confident. "Have you ever had a personal experience of sexual violence?" she asked.

I hesitated, uncomfortable with the directness of the question and its conflict with my desire to maintain a positive spin. I also understood she was looking to me as someone she could trust, who would not evade tough questions and would tell it like it is. Such qualities in a facilitator were important for imparting assurance to those who felt uncertain or frightened.

I retreated from my lecture position at the front of the group and sat in the circle with the women. Taking a deep breath, I replied, "Yes." I then told my story in public for the first time. I thought I would feel unsteady and break into tears. Instead, I was keenly aware of the group's rapt attention, their sudden need to know, and their subsequent understanding that I was there as an example of empowerment so that they could in turn empower themselves.

After that moment, I noticed a marked change in the group's personal commitment and camaraderie as they participated in class exercises. When we began learning skills and techniques, the women were genuinely invested in their endeavors: standing with confidence, speaking assertively, and courageously defending their personal boundaries. And they encouraged and cheered one another's heroic acts, their solidarity palpable.

The emotional power of this experience helped me understand that fear, which I had strictly relegated to only one side of my proverbial coin, could morph more easily into empowerment if I released the white-knuckled hold on my own emotion and allowed for its natural expression. In future workshops, I chose to face my fear and share my story, even allowing myself to cry. Sometimes tears would well up, but far from being a distraction, they seemed a healthy release that gave others permission to connect with their own fear and somehow—almost incredibly—begin the process of transforming it.

10

Emotions

It's been said that we teach what we most need to learn; this was the case for me during my years of facilitating the assertiveness workshops. I was passionately drawn to women who were willing to explore the edge of their comfort zone, push themselves to find their voice, and aspire to stand in their power. In hindsight, I see that attempting to assure confidence and safety for other women was a way to satisfy my desire to control what felt uncontrollable: my incessant fear and anxiety. What I'd overlooked were key components of a more holistic approach to confidence: the emotional and spiritual aspects of experience. But at the time, these were not only less familiar parts of my reality; I also believed they had no scientific or intellectual validity. I viewed them as less significant and unworthy of my time and energy.

So while facilitating the workshops empowered me, it also depleted me. As women shared their personal stories and anxieties, I was besieged with multiple mirrors of concern, anger, and fear—all of which triggered my inner alarm, making me painfully aware of the discord within me. Outside the workshops, my anxiety surfaced as shortness of breath, edginess in personal interactions, and wakeful nights before teaching. As well, I had continuing trouble with my hips; demonstrating a positive stance and walk often caused them to seize up, making forward movement stiff and painful. Participants were not likely to notice, but I had to move cautiously and slowly. I felt frustrated that my body seemed at odds with my mission.

During this time, Tom and I were working to start a family. We'd been married three years when, in July of 1996, we learned we were pregnant. Four months later, our excitement as new parents-to-be was met with disappointment when I miscarried.

The loss caught me off guard, but I denied myself the opportunity to grieve by rationalizing my discomfort. I convinced myself the timing wasn't right and that the loss was a blessing that would reveal its gifts at some point in the future. The miscarriage was unfortunate, but no one was seriously hurt, and time would heal my disappointment.

To imagine expressing my grief felt ominous; if I uncapped the bottle, my emotions might spew uncontrollably. It would be messy, and there was no telling how long it could last. But keeping it inside compounded my emotional burden, until it eventually found voice through the increasing pain in my hips and pelvis.

It was two years before I became pregnant again. I wanted to do things differently this time, to prevent a similar result, so I worked hard to shift my priorities and perspectives. I gradually stepped back from my assertiveness trainings. That genre of work wasn't gentle, and I sensed the imbalance of combining that vocation with motherhood. I felt more guarded in the second pregnancy, not sharing the news until I was six months pregnant—just to be sure it was going to stick. I made a point to walk daily in a nearby arboretum, which offered me both solace and strength, and I relieved stress by taking a spin on my bicycle. As my belly grew, so did my desire to embrace the experience of pregnancy, listen more intently to my changing body, and nurture myself. Perhaps these were the gifts that grew out of the miscarriage.

As excited as I was to be pregnant, my body suffered for it. My breathing issues faded to the background as my hips, under the pressure of added baby weight, commanded my attention. It was my left hip that held the core of the pain, with tentacles like octopus arms reaching out to my sacrum, over to my right hip, and down the length of my left leg even into my toes, delivering dreadfully sharp pulsations to one or more of these areas. Just like the giant cephalopod, my pain would occasionally squeeze itself into a space so tiny—my hip joint or big toe, for example—that it would become nearly imperceptible; then, as I rose to my feet or attempted to walk, I'd be overcome with the immensity of its presence.

My primary care doctor referred me to an orthopedic specialist, in whose office I had to wait over two hours to be seen. The doctor then delivered the prognosis that I was the most flexible person he'd ever met, that my hip X-rays looked a little odd, but that no, he didn't see any way to help me.

Discouraged, and somewhat disgusted with the inability of modern medicine to provide at least a little insight, I committed to finding an alternative path to healing. I tried myofascial release, yoga therapy, network chiropractic, and multiple other modalities. While each provided temporary relief, there seemed no permanent fix. Both traditional and alternative therapists agreed on one thing: there was no obvious explanation for my pain. Sure, I had tightness here, imbalance there, and was offered stretches, strengthening exercises, and a myriad of energetic and holistic remedies. Because the discomfort had appeared shortly after the rape, I linked my pain with the trauma, and as time progressed, this association felt undeniable. In retrospect, I wish I'd sought more medical opinions and pressed more proactively for a solution. Instead, the path I chose led to increased discomfort.

At that point, nurturing and self-compassion were not my defining attributes. I remember a rainy evening upon my return from a meditation retreat. I had placed a take-out order for Tom and me at our favorite Japanese restaurant. When I stopped by for pickup, it wasn't ready. The hostess, a small, gentle Asian woman, approached me as I sat waiting.

"Can I bring you a cup of hot tea while you wait?" she asked.

Perhaps it was the genuine kindness in her voice or just that single nurturing act, but her query instantly brought me to tears. I sat on the black vinyl chair, my face as wet and droopy as my raincoat. Her willingness to care for me seemed to speak directly to the part of me that desperately longed for nurturing. For years, my focused, driven self hadn't allowed me to even consider accepting such an offer. In that moment, I realized I could choose to be supported. Not only did I accept the tea, but I sat waiting long after my take-out order was handed to me. For that brief time, I abandoned my usual pushing and haste and simply enjoyed a small gift.

What is now clear to me is that my continued tolerance of pain and discomfort further desensitized me to my emotional experience. I saw several talk therapists during this period, with the sole intent of restoring physical comfort, not of understanding my emotional landscape. My hampered breathing and the persistent burning pain down the length of my left leg were causing increased frustration, and I wanted nothing more than to discover the source of my affliction, learn some ways to address it, and achieve physical comfort and inner peace. I'd have rather avoided emotions, but my primary therapist had other plans. She soon had me engaged in Eye Movement Desensitization and Reprocessing (EMDR) therapy, which seemed a gentle and effective way of working with emotions to reduce my overall distress surrounding the trauma.

Throughout, I don't know that I ever considered my emotions "the enemy," but they were certainly not "my friends." Their unpredictable and vexatious behavior was an annoyance that increasingly required attention and focus, and I didn't want to take time for them. In my exploration of healing modalities, I continued to evade the emotional repository where dwelt a growing beast of festering disturbance. I became skilled at pushing myself forward through anxiety, discomfort, fear, and acute pain. This strategy kept me seemingly safe but also numb.

My husband will tell you he remembers this period as the beginning of my descent into darkness and detachment. The pain and angst monopolized my energy, leaving little for him and our son, Joseph. As Tom describes it, I became like a heat-seeking missile in search of healing. It was an obsession that separated me from my family and from my sense of purpose or livelihood, and it impacted Tom in ways I'll never fully know. Through it all, Tom was my steady; he stood beside me, offering unflinching support for each step I took in pursuit of greater balance and strength.

Gradually, with the support of my health practitioners, I began to understand that my health extended beyond my physical body. A holistic view of health included emotional well-being and the inner harmony established through spiritual practice. My pain and angst, I was told, were likely expressions of an inner imbalance. My emotions and spirit needed support and nurturing as much as my physical body.

"Often, our thoughts or beliefs will affect our emotional

well-being," my acupuncturist said. "Our emotions, in turn, affect our physical well-being. I'm not saying that you'll be well if you change your thoughts, but it's a piece of the puzzle. You may want to look beyond your specific physical challenges and examine what other parts of your life are not working. There may be a correlation."

Her words felt true to me, and in the weeks that followed, I explored what else in my life needed attention. Previous to the trauma, I had felt clear and passionate about my work in the classroom. Teaching chemistry had seemed a perfect fit for me; chemistry held both certainty and mystery, a combination I found captivating and provocative. In my science teaching enclave, I had seeming control over incidents that might otherwise appear surprising or unexpected. I knew formulas that explained at the particle or energy level what happened during a fizz, a color change, an explosion. Once I identified the reagents or reacting substances of a chemical reaction, I could more easily predict the resulting products. I loved knowing the imperceptible subtleties that produced visible and sometimes incredible outcomes.

In my experience outside of the classroom, the rape had been an unexpected reagent that was added to the mix; it had scrambled my life. My passion for teaching chemistry had waned in the shadow of trauma, and I'd concluded there were more important things for young people to learn than science. How to stay safe was one of them. However, having abandoned my assertiveness training workshops and taken on the responsibilities of motherhood, I soon felt small and without direction and a clear purpose. My facilitation work had been the most meaningful work to which I'd since committed. And with my energy fully directed toward mothering a budding family, I quickly determined I didn't want my life to be focused solely on dinner and diapers.

Emotions

I remembered a younger me who felt invincible and full of promise as I'd toured and commuted alone on my bicycle. Being raped seemed to have frozen some part of me in time, leaving a void. The part of me that was passionate and focused in my work and spunky and strong in my play was missing. "Feeling well" began to take on a more expanded meaning. I was soon seeking "wholeness," something more than physical and mental well-being, something that included meaning and purpose in life.

While the stress of pain and angst often felt overwhelming, I can now see the grace in being pushed to my limit. In my desperation, I became increasingly open to trying new things. I began considering additional factors that might support greater ease—some reagents without which desired results could not form.

A close friend encouraged me to try something called applied kinesiology. She'd received this treatment for years and had numerous success stories. The process was simple, she said—testing the body's muscles for strength or weakness in order to diagnose imbalances and suggest treatment. Her practitioner, Dr. Pat, a chiropractor and kinesiologist, was just a few miles from our home.

Dr. Pat, I soon learned, was known by many as the go-to doctor for long-standing ailments with no apparent remedy. He had a reputation for successfully moving people from chronic pain and illness to greater balance and health. Though I found it challenging to quiet my inner skeptic, my desperation won out, and I scheduled an appointment.

Dr. Pat's office was small and orderly. Tiny vials lined small white shelves on the walls surrounding the treatment table. The vials were labeled with printed tags citing names of molds and fungus, candida, pollens, all types of foods, as well as toxins such as mercury and other heavy metals. Unlike traditional doctors, Dr. Pat was dressed comfortably in khakis, a blue sport shirt, and loafers. He was considerate and patient, taking the time to ask plenty of questions, to feel into my responses, and to assure he had covered all possibilities.

Dr. Pat had me lie on the table while he plucked various vials from the display, held them near my head, and pushed on my upheld arm. He moved purposefully, methodically, checking groups of vials and narrowing down to one or two that had the most profound muscle response. This technique, he said, told him which substances caused my muscles to become weak. A weak muscle response to one of the vials indicated my sensitivity to what was in it. Other vials held homeopathic remedies that could produce a strengthened response from my muscles; these became part of my treatment. The testing provided Dr. Pat with a greater understanding of the source of my illness and helped him formulate a path to address it.

"It's interesting," he remarked after a round of muscle testing, "that it's your left hip that's so distressed. The left side of the body typically represents our feminine aspect. So, I suspect something has severely wounded the feminine part of you. Does that feel true?"

I hadn't told him about the rape. Having just met him, I didn't feel comfortable sharing intimate information, and I wasn't sure it was pertinent. But I could feel his concern and sincere desire to help.

"Yes, that feels true for me," I replied in quieter than normal tones. "I was raped several years ago, and I just can't seem to work past the effects of the trauma."

"Gosh, I'm sorry you've had to deal with that," he said. "It makes sense to me then that you're experiencing the achiness and what appears to be adrenal fatigue. These symptoms tell me that you would benefit from self-care, and from releasing pent-up emotions. This type of trauma can understandably produce anxiety and excessive burden. What's concerning is that you don't want your body to be under this type of stress for very long."

"I don't want to be," I said, "but I can't seem to get out of pain."

Dr. Pat paused, seeming to consider something. Then he looked at me, his eyes intense and purposeful. I felt a little intimidated by his directness.

"This is going to require a new way of being with yourself, Anne. It's possible to heal, but you need to know that this is not just about eliminating symptoms."

I latched onto the words "It's possible to heal" and felt the relief of them filling my weary body. The remainder of his counsel drifted away.

He continued. "With any illness, there's an underlying cause, something emotionally or spiritually rooted, that's calling for our attention. This is going to require you to listen to your emotional and spiritual needs and nurture yourself."

Self-indulgent popped into my thoughts. *Not needed, don't have the time for it.* But some inner voice nudged me so strongly that I felt elbowed in the ribs. It told me to pay attention to what I'd just been told.

"Could you repeat that?" I asked Dr. Pat as tears flooded my eyes.

"Yes, you're going to need to take good care of yourself, Anne. Be present with what you need, listen to your body, and respond with support."

I felt confused and overwhelmed with emotion. His words sounded foreign to me. I wasn't certain what self-care looked like, but I trusted Dr. Pat and was willing to give it a try.

Though I was less familiar with the emotional and spiritual domains he referred to, I assumed they operated logically and with a practical method or formula I could comprehend. *Once*

I know the proper equation, I thought, *and plug in its variables, it will be just a matter of time before I reach a solution.* But as soon as that thought appeared, I recognized it as my old way of thinking. I'd already experienced the unpredictability of emotions, the mystery of spirit; if there was a system to emotions and spirituality, it wasn't coherent. Sensing my journey was about to become messy in a completely different way, I saw nothing better to do than take a deep breath and roll up my pant legs.

I began by studying ancient energy practices that influence the healing process. A friend introduced me to qigong and tai chi, holistic methods to improve mental and physical health through integration of posture, movement, breathing, and intent. I took classes from local practitioners to learn the basics of these ancient arts. One of the qigong instructors introduced me to some recorded talks that related bodily organs with emotions and offered cleansing meditations as a path to healing, and I began to incorporate listening and meditation into my daily routine. Another friend invited me to a lecture by a woman who emphasized the importance of forgiveness on the path to healing; this also became part of my daily regimen. It seemed simple enough to adopt new practices to take care of my emotions, but in my zealous and naive pursuit, I soon discovered another oversight: I would be required to release my hold on certainty and control—two elements intrinsic to my existence.

11

Possibility

W hoa! They're everywhere!" I said as I spied kitchen counters and cabinets covered with tiny crawling insects. I was six years old.

Mom was scurrying about, trying to brush the little bodies onto paper and carefully place them outdoors. There were hundreds of them.

Several days prior, my older brother, Paul, and I had discovered a cocoon hanging on a bush in our side yard. Curious about the butterfly that would emerge, we snapped the limb and carried the cocoon into the house. Mom got an empty mason jar from the pantry and plopped the twig with its crusty beige dwelling into the opening. We forgot about it until the morning we woke to crowds of baby mantises clouding our kitchen.

Another time, when I was seven or eight, Dad was mowing our front lawn and disrupted a nest of rabbits near the edge of the yard. With his worn leather garden gloves, he gathered up three baby bunnies and brought them to me for safekeeping while he finished his work. I lined my plastic bike basket with soft green grass, gently placed the bunnies in their new mobile bungalow, and taxied them up and down our driveway for hours, stopping often to touch their soft fur.

Though I was a studious child and excelled at academics, I also enjoyed rich and magical interactions with nature. Whether it was the black snakes we rescued from the strawberry net, the passageways I explored amongst the brambles near our home, or the wild black raspberries we harvested on the edge of our property each June, these childhood experiences formed the foundation for me to expect the unexpected, to know that life could take sudden and astonishing turns and reveal something marvelous.

Nevertheless, miracles—transformations that could not be explained by science—were a concept I warmed to cautiously. My mind required a rational basis or personal experience to give credence to something beyond reason. However, the faint and timid whisper of my heart fiercely believed in miracles. It was this heart whisper that began to speak to me in my despairing moments during the years I sought healing. It was this quiet voice that encouraged me to stay open to possibility.

Crowds of participants gathered on the beach side of the resort, the half moon and stars lighting the night sky. Tom and I were two of hundreds. Through Tom's work, he had an opportunity to attend a personal development seminar. Upon learning of it, my heart began to nudge me to attend with him, so I made plans to do so. We'd committed to this experience not fully knowing what would be presented to—or expected of—us. Having signed an imposing waiver at registration that indicated we couldn't sue for injury or loss of life, I felt I'd made a leap and was waiting for my feet to hit solid ground. The only reassuring thought about my decision was that it had clearly satisfied my heart whisper.

Forty feet of red coals spanned before us. We'd been preparing for this encounter for hours in the seminar hall, coached and inspired by the facilitator. Now the crowd was silent, each of us maintaining inner focus while we waited our turn. The movement of the line was tortoise-like, people winding circuitously across the resort lawn and toward the coals that were spread near the beach. As we came closer, I heard the yelps and whoops of excitement from those who were walking or had just walked a fiery forty feet. I focused inward, affirming my strength, my certainty that I could walk barefoot across the expanse of burning embers.

Firewalking has been practiced for thousands of years by people of many cultures and in all parts of the world. It's often used as a rite of passage, a test of strength or courage, or in religious circles, as a test of faith. In this seminar the firewalk was used as an experiential metaphor for creating breakthroughs and overcoming fears. I set the bar high for myself, choosing an intention to release any fear I held and stepping fully toward work to empower others. I wanted desperately to teach others how to navigate life without fear. I knew on some level this would mean facing my own fear, addressing it, and setting the example for others. I was ready for the challenge and had strong incentive to get to the other side of whatever deterred me. The fire's temper seemed mitigated with my determination.

Burning coals exceed one thousand degrees Fahrenheit. Physicists claim the secret of the firewalk lies in the low thermal conductivity of the burning wood and the short span of time that hot coals make contact with the surface of the feet. Regardless of any scientific explanation, I was sweating profusely before setting foot on the embers. Perhaps this was due partly to some anxiety, but the heat from the coals was enough to redden my face. In my meditative state, time seemed compressed, and soon my feet met the luminous threshold. It was my turn to transform any inner doubts into strong life-giving convictions.

A Fierce Belief in Miracles

I have all I need within me. I release any and all fears and stand in my strength ready to empower myself and others, I repeated silently to myself. Part of our preparation for this moment was to hold strong intent—a compelling reason to move forward. I stood with certainty and fortitude for a brief moment, then stepped confidently onto the coals.

Cool moss, cool moss, cool moss, I repeated silently as I stepped quickly but deliberately across the coals. This mantra had been suggested as we were led in our preparatory pursuit of "mind over matter."

The crunchy surface shifted slightly as I walked forward; I kept my eyes focused on the smooth surface of cool sand just beyond the pyre. When my toes sank into the soft, sandy ground, I felt elated, relieved, and intensely powerful. Perhaps this accomplishment had nothing to do with mind over matter, but the effect was, nonetheless, poignant. I had just completed something that hours before I didn't believe I could do. And there I was, on the other side—capable, steady, and unharmed.

If I could walk across fire, I most certainly could walk through life without fear. I also felt certain I could transform my pain and angst into comfort and peace. But this wouldn't be a mundane endeavor. The firewalk had required intense preparation, clear vision, and an openness to possibility. It was the possibility that enticed me. The firewalk had revealed a sort of spiritual alchemy. I had focused on a possibility, stepped into the unknown, and transcended primal fear. I had—perhaps for the first time—consciously and confidently chosen faith to deliver me to the other side of something formidable. What's more, there was an identifiable pattern to the process—a formula for miracles, albeit an unconventional one: (1) listen to my heart's urging, (2) take action with confidence and certainty, and (3) trust.

12

Opening

The formula for miracles was challenging to put into practice. I wasn't always clear whether the voice I heard was my rational self or my emotional and spiritual self. With no control over outcomes, I felt hesitant taking steps directed only by instinct or intuition. When I didn't have much to risk, I'd experiment, but the results weren't always satisfactory. I was charmed by my inner knowing yet at the same time wanted to impose reason. These distinct forces often seemed to compete, and I'd end up feeling misguided or silly.

One summer, traveling home from vacation, Tom and I were hungry for lunch and had pulled off the interstate onto a long side road passing warehouses, an occasional residential area, and a couple of small strip malls. It was before we had access to the Internet and applications such as Yelp, so we weren't certain where to find a decent meal.

Always encouraging, Tom half-jokingly coaxed me. "Feel into it, Anne, and tell me which way we should turn at the next intersection to find a delicious lunch."

I laughed briefly but then felt a definite pull to my right. "Right, I'm feeling right," I replied with confidence.

At the light, we turned right and found ourselves amidst more of the same. I began feeling uncertain, and we joked about how long we wanted to devote to this lunch break as we followed my intuitive navigation system.

"I'm not skilled at this, Tom. Let's just stop and ask someone."

"No, I'm trusting you on this," he replied, and continued down the road.

What felt like ten minutes later, we did happen upon an area that looked more promising, with some shops and small restaurants. By then I was fairly discouraged, but Tom rallied with, "You see? You are skilled at this."

"I don't know," I said. "Anything will show up if you drive long enough."

But with Tom's continued prompting, my own intermittent experimentation, and some levity, I began to trust my inner guidance.

As it happened, it was about this time that Tom took on the position of Vice President of the Appalachian Chapter of the American Society of Dowsers. His primary job was to secure speakers for upcoming events. This opened the door for us both to get to know skilled and well-known dowsers and healers and to participate in their workshops. The list of presenters that I came to know and respect included Harold McCoy, author of *Power of Focused Mind Healing* and founder of the Ozark Research Institute, an educational organization promoting healing and spiritual awakening through holistic research; Dorothy Maclean, one of the founders of the Findhorn Foundation, which promotes inner listening and co-creation with the intelligence of nature; and Joey Korn, world-renowned dowser and author of *Dowsing: A Path to Enlightenment*, with emphasis on using prayer and blessing to create harmony in ourselves and the world.

Dowsing or divining is the use of an instrument (usually rods or a pendulum) as a conduit for our subconscious knowledge or perception. Some say the instrument creates a bridge between the logical and intuitive parts of the brain. Primarily known as a method to find water, dowsing can be used to find all sorts of things. The art is in asking the right questions or directing our subconscious in a clear way. Dowsing is not so much about finding something tangible as it is about tapping into our innate ability to explore the world of subtle energies that are everywhere within and around us.

With my background in chemistry, I had a good understanding of energy systems. I knew from quantum mechanics that at the subatomic level, everything is energy. So I understood the idea that when you dowse for water, you're detecting the energy field of the water rather than the water itself. Just as radios pick up information from unseen waves, dowsing devices are antennas that receive information from the energy waves emitted by people, places, and things. The process of dowsing for something—water, clarity, balance, health—relies on creating a resonant vibration within ourselves by visualizing and feeling what we seek.

Skeptical of the concept at the outset, I began by observing other dowsers, taking classes, and practicing what I learned. After witnessing repeated positive outcomes, I couldn't totally discount the practice. In one instance, my family was experiencing significant difficulty with a new neighbor who was both loud and disrespectful of our property. Their young son had begun coming to play in our backyard and was using foul language. I let him know that he was welcome at our home but his foul language was not. The next day, his parents came to our door with an ax in hand to introduce themselves. This situation definitely called for a shift in energy.

I began doing the energy dowsing and healing blessings I'd been taught to remedy such situations. Though the boy stopped coming to our home, the family's loud music and raucous nightly behavior continued without noticeable change. I contacted my dowsing teacher Joey Korn and asked for his help. Working virtually by dowsing our property via Google Maps, he confirmed that my blessings had energetically protected our property boundary.

"You've done a good job with what I've taught you," Joey said over the phone. "However, I find some core centers of detrimental energy on the neighboring property. It appears these energies were set up many years ago. Any chance that these people had a connection to this land before moving in?"

"Yes, they're extended family of folks who've lived in this neighborhood for years," I said.

"That makes sense," he confirmed. "And this isn't something you could have found with the training you've received, but it's what needs to be balanced in order for the energy to shift."

"Can you take care of this?" I asked.

"Already did," he replied. "Should be fine now, so expect to see a shift."

Within forty-eight hours, the family next door had moved away. We never saw them again. I immediately signed up for Joey's next five-day intensive training so I could learn more about his work.

Connections I made and teachers I met through the local dowsing group opened a door to deeper exploration of energy, spirituality, and healing—topics I'd previously lumped in a category I called "magic." I began to give more attention and credence to my intuitive sense; soon, intuition was less "magic" and more a renewed connection with part of me that I'd disregarded for years.

My newfound intuitive awareness was likely accentuated by the fact I was a new mother; motherhood was an emotional journey that was exhilarating, exhausting, and sometimes scary. Allowing myself to feel more feelings than I was accustomed to created an opening that began to affect my dreams and imagination.

My nighttime dreamscape became unusually active, and I'd often wake feeling I'd traveled far away while sleeping. Occasionally I'd write down the details of a dream that felt potent or meaningful, but more often I considered dreams part of an active imagination and disregarded them. In truth, motherhood was taxing; I had little time or energy to devote much attention to dreams. That is, until the angel appeared.

It was summertime. Tom was on a five-day business trip to Atlanta. This left me home alone with Joseph, who was less than a year old. I didn't mind being alone; in fact, I enjoyed having the house to myself and feeling more independent in how I structured my days. I was, at that time, always tired and slept hard at night.

I was sleeping soundly on my belly—"drool-sleep," I called it—when I was awakened by footsteps in our bedroom. In my dreamy state, I thought Tom had come in. He often worked into the evening and most nights came to bed after I'd been sleeping a couple of hours. I felt content knowing he was coming to bed. I lay on my belly, my body heavy with sleep, while my attentive ear followed the sound of footsteps on the wood floor down the side of the room to the foot of the bed, where they stopped. *It couldn't be Tom. He's out of town*, I suddenly realized. My body grew tense, my heartbeat frenzied. A few seconds expanded to long minutes as my perception slowed.

Someone was standing at the foot of our bed. My body began to perspire. I lay still and flat, trying to make myself imperceptible. I listened, trying to hear anything—breath, movement. *What is the intruder doing?* I focused my energy, took a deep breath, and with one brisk movement, flipped my body over. I sat up, squinting at the foot of the bed. The faint moonlight from the window lit the room enough to reveal nothing—no one was there.

I flicked on the bedside table light and looked around the room. Nothing. Slipping out of bed, I opened the door and tiptoed across the hall to check on Joseph. Fine. Sleeping. I was still shaking, still certain something or someone had walked into my room. *It must have been a vivid dream,* I reasoned. It took a while to fall back to sleep.

About an hour after this occurrence, again in deep sleep, I wakened to the sound of our bedroom door opening, then footsteps. This time I realized more quickly it couldn't be Tom. I was tired but fully awake as I lay on my stomach, sweating profusely under my blanket. The person stopped at the side of the bed—*my* side of the bed. I felt the mattress sink as the person sat down next to me. Then the person leaned in, the mattress sinking deeper, and a hand gently touched my shoulder. I zipped around, ready to do battle, only to find an empty room. *What was it? What just happened? Who was there?* The clock read 5:00 a.m. *Perhaps something has happened to Tom; I should check on him.* Frightened and unsettled, I called Tom in Atlanta. Besides being awakened uncomfortably early, he was fine.

"I'm willing to head home," he said.

"No. I'm okay. I've just had a rough night."

That day I directed my energy toward figuring out how to prevent this from happening again. I called Robert, the husband of a good friend.

"I have a favor to ask of you," I said hesitantly.

Opening

"What can I do for you?"

"This may sound strange, but I was awakened last night by what I thought was a person walking in my room. I know this sounds crazy, but Tom's out of town, and I'm feeling uneasy about going to sleep tonight."

"Would you like to stay at our home?" he offered.

"Thanks. I feel it's best for me to stay here, but I'm wondering if you'd be willing to be on call for me should this happen again," I said.

"Sure. Call anytime, day or night. I'm happy to come over if you need me to," he assured me.

Comforted that I had someone to call, I thanked him. Then I went about the task of contacting others—alternative health-care practitioners, intuitives, friends, and psychics—to gain clarity on what had happened and to assure that I wouldn't lose another night's sleep to elusive visitors. Most of my contacts had no answers; some likely thought I'd lost my mind. One person scolded me for "playing around with spirits." That was not a message I needed at the time. I wanted to find someone who could help me comfortably connect with the presence that had obviously appeared to engage with me. It was my acupuncturist who provided the most helpful suggestion.

"If you're frightened, you can tell this spirit—or whatever it is—that you need your sleep. Request that it not visit you at night," she offered. "Just light a candle in the evening and create a safe space by calling in spirits of love and light. Ask for their protection. Then call in the one that visited you last night and speak to it directly, telling it what you want."

This was all new to me. I wasn't one for ceremonies and had never directly addressed a spirit of this sort, but I was desperate for a good night's rest and knew I needed something to help me feel safe enough to close my eyes.

That evening, just after sunset, I pulled a fat red Christmas candle out of the hall closet, placed it on an old pottery plate, lit it with a wooden match, and sat with its warm glow in the middle of the brown carpet in the living room.

"All beings of love and light," I began awkwardly, "please come join me in my home and provide protection for me." Then, somewhat hesitantly, I continued, "I'm requesting of the spirit that came into my bedroom last night to not come visit me while I'm sleeping. I need my rest and prefer that you connect with me during daylight while I'm awake."

I had said what needed saying. I sat silently in the candlelight. As I glanced to the side, I noticed, rising from behind the couch, a large orange ball of light. I didn't move, not even to take a breath. It ascended to about a foot above the couch and hovered there for a minute, glowing with intensity, and certainly with purpose. The entire room was filled with some unfamiliar yet loving presence. My body was embraced wholly, fully, by some giant warmhearted being, and I felt suddenly relaxed, safe, and unconditionally supported. It was as if the message was "I'm here to support you. You haven't been paying attention to this resource, and it's time to open yourself to it." Then, like a breath that had rushed in, it rushed out and I was left with only my burning candle.

For days after, I felt the warm glow of that experience come into my awareness on various occasions—late evenings as I lay in bed, in a quiet kitchen as I prepared dinner, and mostly in my morning meditation. I began referring to the visitor as "my angel," and my beliefs and perspectives began to shift. Skepticism was no longer my initial response to spiritual phenomena. Instead, I grew curious about metaphysical topics and wanted to understand how these other realities could mesh with my own.

As well, I was able to take a closer look at my fear. While the angel's appearance felt like it was offering me guidance or support, its presentation had been frightening. For weeks, I could only sleep if the lamp on my bedside table was burning through the night. I began experimenting with my emotion to see how it might change things. At bedtime, I would lie on my back, focus on my heart, and imagine sharing loving energy with the visitor I feared. As I quieted my mind holding this intent, I felt the same full body embrace I'd felt that evening in the living room. Gradually it became easier to connect with something I could only feel, not see. And I began to appreciate and enjoy this spiritual presence in my life.

As I settled into more frequent angelic connections, I began to feel my angel's arrival was a direct appeal from the other side to pay attention and listen to something, though I wasn't sure what. I resolved to figure it out. I began reading books and articles about spiritual encounters and mystical experience. I discovered a woman who'd received her science degrees from Duke University and had been visited by angels in her pediatric oncology lab. Her impressive credentials inspired me to hear her speak. Though researching and connecting with others' stories was affirming for me, it didn't offer insight into what *my* angel wanted to communicate.

Though my focus was on things esoteric and mysterious, my days were burdened with increased pain and stress. In addition to grocery shopping, meal preparation, laundry, and caring for my sweet boy, I was nursing each night. With little sleep, I soon found myself exhausted to the extent that it was hard to imagine how I'd previously been able get up out of a chair or walk easily across a room. My energy and my spirit began to fade as I pushed myself to meet the demands of being a new mom. My joints ached continuously, my breathing was compromised more frequently, and I was more prone to tears and upset.

I decided to return to Dr. Pat. He'd helped me before, and I felt confident he'd help me again.

"You're showing sensitivity to barium sulfate," he said after a round of muscle testing. "This is a common component of root canal fillings."

The punch in my face by the rapist had severely damaged the nerves to two of my teeth, and they eventually required root canals.

"So I'm reacting in a negative way to those fillings?"

"Yes, you need to get those redone. I'd recommend filling them with gutta-percha. It's an inert substance and will make a significant improvement in your health. Not only do I expect you'll have more energy and emotional balance, but it could very likely help the pain in your hips and legs."

"So you're telling me that my exhaustion, pain, and anxiety are due to my teeth?" I was in disbelief. "I'm not sure I understand how that could be."

"Teeth nine and ten, those currently with root canals, are related by energy meridians to your hips and legs, as well as to the pineal gland. This meridian system addresses hormonal balance, which would affect your sleep. It's also related to emotional disturbance, instability, fear, and moodiness."

It sounded suspect to me, but he was clearly describing my current challenges.

"You may also want to research the pineal gland," he continued, knowing my interest in understanding it all. "The pineal is known to play an important role in spiritual experience. I know we haven't explored anything about spirituality, but I thought you'd like to know."

"Wow. That's curious," I replied. I wasn't sure what else to say. *Would Dr. Pat think I'd lost my marbles if I told him about the angel?* I chose to keep that episode to myself for the moment, but I was beginning to sense the interconnectedness of it all.

At home, I researched the pineal gland. I learned that it's located at the center of the brain, behind and above the pituitary gland. The pineal gland is the body's primary source of melatonin, and its health and balance affect our mood, immune function, circadian rhythms, and the quality and quantity of our sleep. And sure enough, it's on the same energy meridian as the musculature of the lower extremities. When the pineal gland is activated, it secretes consciousness-expanding biochemicals believed by ancient spiritual traditions to open the third eye of inner vision, insight, and wisdom.

I phoned my dentist to schedule replacement fillings for my root canals.

13

Miracles

After the angel visitation, I found myself entranced by the realm apart from physical reality that seemed filled with mystery or magic. I was desperately hoping to learn that life was enchanted, because I couldn't fathom a way out of my painful situation without the existence of miracles. Miracles, large or small, would dispense enough optimism for me to visualize myself walking with ease and strength.

My hip pain didn't seem relieved by the root canal work; however, I was glad I'd done it. Just taking the action—clearing out one potential source of imbalance—produced a lightness and clarity I'd not felt in a while. Whether placebo or simply the act of self-care, I was grateful to experience a greater sense of peace.

Three years after the angel visit, I was pregnant with my second child, a daughter. My already faltering pelvis was further compromised by the pregnancy, which challenged me from the beginning. The shift in hormones and the softening of muscles and ligaments around my pelvis destabilized my hips, making me feel unsteady on my feet.

Miracles

Though I had difficulty walking, I could still ride my bike comfortably because cycling didn't put pressure on the hip joints. When I could get away from family responsibilities, I'd drive my bike to the parkway, park at an overlook, and ride until I felt fulfilled. I'd return home calm and renewed. Cycling diverted my attention from what wasn't working and lifted my spirits.

The angel encounter had not only ushered in more optimism about my painful situation but also opened the door to spiritual sources of support. I was soon introduced to the local Center for Spiritual Living, its core teaching being Science of Mind. Founded by Ernest Holmes in 1926, Science of Mind affirms that our intentions or prayers flow as energy through a field of consciousness which, in turn, determines our experience. According to this philosophy, the formula for a happy, healthy life is to consciously affirm positive outcomes in our thoughts. I was skeptical about the doctrine but appreciated the simplicity of the formula and was willing to test it out.

It felt good to be part of a community practicing faithful optimism. In addition to attending Sunday service, I soon committed to a multiyear training to become a Science of Mind Practitioner—someone trained in the skill of spiritual mind treatment or affirmative prayer. As I increased my awareness of the interactions among my body, mind, and spirit and learned to recognize and release fears, I began to experience more flow and ease in my life. I was hopeful that training my mind and controlling my focus would create a different and more positive experience. I thought if I could master this practice, I'd be well on my way to ease and wholeness.

For four years I attended evening classes, met with study groups, and engaged in thoughtful writing and dialogue. Paired with fellow practitioners-in-training, we offered one another affirmative prayer, celebrated positive outcomes, and deepened friendships. In class we shared stories of healed relationships, health restored, doctors awed by rapid healing, and numerous uncanny synchronicities.

My own practice with affirmative prayer began by setting goals that felt probable. Though I'd often achieve my outcome, I could easily discount it as coincidence. When I set my sights on improbable goals but didn't achieve them through affirmative prayer, I'd question my method or wonder if this was a futile practice altogether. The occasional miraculous outcome, however, began to build a foundation for my faith.

One such miracle happened during my pregnancy. Toward the end of my second trimester, our doctor recommended that I get an ultrasound. It was standard procedure for pregnant women over forty, he said. At the clinic, Tom and I sat in the treatment room while the technician performed the ultrasound. The doctor asked to meet with us afterward.

The scan, he said, revealed that our daughter had polydactyly, a condition in which a person has more than her fair share of fingers. Along with the doctor, we examined the pictures. Sure enough, there were six fully formed fingers on each hand, the extra digits appearing next to the pinky fingers. My heart sank.

"What does this mean?" I asked. "Will she be okay?"

"Likely so," he replied, "but we can't know for certain. Polydactyly can be associated with a number of other birth defects, some of which can be identified through amniocentesis, others not. Amnio's a riskier procedure than ultrasound, and obviously it'll be your choice if you'd like to go through with it."

The news left me unsettled and anxious. My pregnancy, now clouded with concern, would have me waiting at least another three months before delivery. Tom and I discussed the implications of having the amniocentesis. If we learned something dire at this point in the pregnancy, it wasn't as if we were going to take any actions to end it. The information would prove useful, however, if we discovered something out of the ordinary; it would give us time to prepare ourselves mentally and emotionally for potential challenges. We chose to have the procedure done. No new information came from the amnio, however, and I was left again feeling restless with not knowing.

I called on my practitioner friends to do affirmative prayer for the health of our baby. Nearly a dozen folks included us in their daily spiritual mind treatment, affirming and envisioning the perfection and optimal health of our child. I felt relief knowing my community was supporting us in this way and was amazed that I was able to release my anxiety and enjoy the remainder of my pregnancy.

When she arrived in early October of 2003, Liza was perfect, strong, and healthy. What had appeared in the ultrasound as the sixth fingers were now only tiny flaps of skin. The bones of the extra digits had disappeared completely. I'd have loved every finger and toe on our child regardless of the number, but I was struck with what seemed a significant shift from the ultrasound we'd seen several months ago. This could be interpreted as coincidence, early misdiagnosis, or simply the natural progression of things. However, what I'd seen, heard, and experienced had so clearly transformed into what I desired that it felt beyond any rational explanation. For me, it was a miracle.

While such miracles grounded me in a newfound faith, my personal healing seemed to remain at a standstill. This was incredibly frustrating, yet I did my best to keep my gloomy thoughts out of the equation. Allowing myself to indulge in upset would skew my focus from the positive outcome I desired. Ernest Holmes had taught that our thoughts are our prayers; I believed that directing energy toward my dismay would simply produce more of the same. This fed my belief that emotions were secondary to a logical thought process. In hindsight, I believe that suffocating my emotions likely exacerbated my symptoms.

The mental gymnastics required to manifest a desire soon felt disheartening to me. *Life wasn't meant to be this hard*, I told myself. I asked a teacher at the center for his thoughts on why I hadn't been able to overcome my pain.

"In my experience," he replied, "if the pain in your life is ever-present, there's something else to be learned. I've typically known my pain as a messenger. Perhaps you haven't opened yourself to some part of your experience that wants to be heard or that needs your attention. I'd invite you to consider what that might be."

The words stung a little; I'd been tireless in my pursuit of healing. But I also heard truth in them, and I fiercely wanted to understand what I might be missing. As I allowed myself to consider the teacher's reply more deeply, the first word that popped into my mind was "emotion." I didn't understand its meaning. Emotion, in my experience, was an annoyance—something that got in the way of reaching my goals. I tried to ignore it, but the word kept reappearing in my thoughts.

I sat with that discussion for weeks, asking myself, *What part of my experience wants to be heard or needs my attention?* The answer was repeatedly "emotion." I was soon asking myself, *What do I want to feel?* I wanted to feel the fluidity and vigor of a body that moved easily and painlessly. I equated physical prowess with strength. Currently, I lacked both.

I'd just brought another female into the world, and I wanted to be a powerful role model for her. Liza's ability to embrace inner strength and confidence would be largely dependent on my having done so myself. I wanted the ability to stand tall, to be sure-footed. Though I was primarily looking for physical strength, I sensed I'd find it only if I strengthened some deeply held weakness or fear that was crying out for help.

Miracles

These thoughts inspired a new level of resolve. It was January of 2004 when I reached a moment of conviction. *I would do anything to experience true strength. Anything.* The power of this thought alone made me feel vulnerable, but I knew I'd need to stretch beyond what felt comfortable in order to undergo this seemingly massive change. Feeling ready for the shift, I decided to hold a ceremony. I did as I'd done the evening I spoke with my angel. I lit a candle, stood alone in my living room, invited in helpful spirits, and stated my intention out loud.

"This is my year of strength," I declared aloud, my fists clenched with resolve. "I call on the spiritual realm and on my angel to guide me on the path to rediscover my strength and wholeness." The candle flickered on the coffee table. The silence made me more aware of my senses, and I felt the warmth of a familiar presence. As I relaxed into the angelic embrace, I concluded with a whispered plea. "Please help me know with clarity the direction of my highest good." My words were felt and expressed with my whole being.

Two days later, as I was folding laundry in the living room, I received a phone call from Prince William County. Upon seeing the words highlighted on my caller ID, I felt my body tighten, my breath falter. I answered the phone with hesitation.

"This is Detective Newsome with the Prince William County Police Department. Is this Anne?" His voice was soft and friendly. It was strange hearing that voice—so familiar yet so removed from my present experience. It took me a moment to make the connection. *Newsome. The detective who worked my case. I haven't heard from him in years.* I felt anxious about what he might say next.

"Got a call two days ago from the state prison in West Virginia. There's been a DNA match for your case."

Silence.

My mind and emotions flickered between past and present. Chills ran up my arms. *Two days ago*, I thought, *I affirmed my strength*. I sank onto the couch, spilling freshly folded pants and pillowcases onto the floor, the receiver still tight to my ear. *Fourteen years*. It had been fourteen years since I was brutally attacked and raped.

"The fellow's been charged in a similar case. A West Virginia woman was sexually assaulted in her home the day before you. Same pattern—hit her in the face and raped her. He stole her car."

I wondered about her smile.

The detective spoke with compassion. "This is a lot to digest," he said, "so be good to yourself."

Newsome's voice hung in the air while time seemed suspended, the details of my surroundings somehow melding with his words. *Yes, I'll be good to myself. I'll allow my emotions to settle, ripen like the pears on my counter. Then I'll take small bites to support digestion.* Realizing I'd stopped breathing, I took a deep breath and sighed audibly.

"I'm okay. I'm no longer that emotionally attached," I said, without considering if this was true. I felt lightheaded. "I'm glad they've caught him," I added. "I'll help in any way I can."

The moment I placed the phone down, I was in tears—tears filled with years of contained distress and fear, and now relief and gratitude. I was flooded with feelings, including the anger that I'd linked to this episode for years. I felt a fledgling fear of going to court—or was it excitement? Both felt the same in my body. And his phone call had answered my prayer for strength—I couldn't begin to call it a synchronicity. The enormity of it felt overwhelming. Some power outside of me was definitely responding to my intentions. If what I was seeking was strength, I was certain I was on the right path.

14

Forgiveness

In the chill of winter mornings following the phone call, I woke early, took up my journal, and devoted myself to toiling with words and emotions that would best express the impact the rape had had on my life. Detective Newsome had contacted me again a week later to say that a hearing date had been set for April.

"I'm also calling to ask if you'd be willing to write a victim impact statement for the court. It's not necessary for you to make a statement, but it would likely strengthen our case," he said. I immediately felt drawn to the task. "You could choose to write a statement and have someone else read it in the court-room," he added.

"Yes, I'll write a statement," I replied, "and I'd like to read it myself." I wasn't sure where this would lead, but I was certain it was part of my path to finding strength.

Victim impact statements are typically expected to relay the unfortunate and painful outcomes of a crime. But as I considered it, I knew the outcome for me had encompassed much more. Fourteen years had given me plenty of time to examine the crime and its effect on my life.

A Fierce Belief in Miracles

The word "impact" held dual meaning. There was the impact of the man's fist hitting my face, the impact of his throwing my bike into the bushes, the impact of his body forcing itself into mine. Then there were the blazing sirens that delivered me to the hospital, my body becoming the source of evidence, my swollen face in the mirror, and the pain in friends' faces.

"Impact" also described aspects of my post-rape journey. In the years since the trauma, there was plenty that challenged me, and also much I was grateful for that had come out of that abominable act.

I was impacted by physical pain and emotional struggle and the healing these required. I was impacted by the courageous women I'd met through assertiveness work and by survivors I'd supported in the hospital emergency room. I was impacted by the necessity to stand up for myself and to listen to and express my needs. The rape had required me to stretch in unexpected ways. Its aftermath had ushered in a determination and devotion to healing, emotional self-awareness, and human and spiritual connections I could never have anticipated. How could I possibly communicate the nature and extent of this impact? How could I show what I'd gained from the experience without in any way minimizing such a vicious crime? Though I had done quite a bit of writing over the years, my ability to transform my experience into words for an impact statement seemed as frozen as the ground outside.

That I faltered in defining the true impact of the rape was to be expected. I had, after all, devoted fourteen years to slowly and carefully molding meaning out of the trauma. Being raped is a heinous, ugly, and painful event. As time passed, however, I realized that I had a choice either to focus almost constantly on one or another aspect of the trauma, or to do my best to live in the present moment. The latter was always more life-giving.

However, PTSD in the form of anxiety or hampered breathing often pulled my body and emotions back into trauma, refusing me the comfort I wanted. It took effort to accept that the past and the present were both real.

I'd learned quickly after the rape that I needed to be vigilant about the meaning I assigned to my experience. Early on, I abandoned judgment of the rape as exclusively "bad." Some part of me sensed that over the long term this static interpretation would hinder my healing. With that view removed, the potential existed for the rape itself, and my life afterward, to hold deeper meaning.

I also recognized early on that disclosing my story to others involved risk. Their intense shock, distress, or anger could elicit the same in me, upsetting my still-fluctuating balance. Over years of telling my story, I was continually reminded that safe sharing required discernment.

About four years after moving to Asheville, I had been summoned for jury duty. At the county's judicial complex, I situated myself at a small table with five other people on the edge of a large sitting room as we waited to hear our potential assignments. The group's conversation led to sharing stories of how our lives had been affected by crime. One fellow had his canoe stolen from the edge of a nearby river. A woman spoke of an intruder who'd come into her cousin's apartment. The exchange was animated. I rarely divulged my experience to strangers, but I decided to share that I'd been raped. Talk stopped; people looked at their hands, across the room, at a newspaper. Eventually the silence was interrupted by the woman next to me.

"What the fuck? That sucks!" she exclaimed. "That's a quick path to a ruined life."

Her words launched like a grenade; I wanted to seek cover from the shrapnel. Her anger was intense—after all, we were strangers, I'd thought. Perhaps, though, she was speaking of her own or a loved one's experience. Considering the statistics, it was likely she'd been personally affected by rape. Even so, I instantly retreated to an imaginary foxhole, and my resistance rose to form a defensive front.

Considering the ruin of a life—my life—was a thought I could not afford. Indulging such reflection was a dark alley with no escape, and venturing in was akin to giving away my power. If I claimed the ruin of my life, I could know myself only as a victim.

My life is nowhere near ruined, I affirmed. *My life is full of blessings.* From that moment on, I staked claim on any interpretations of my experience. Only I could assign meaning to what had transpired.

To offset the force of such reactions, I often found myself assuring the listener that all was well, that I had in fact ultimately benefited from the experience. At first, this was an attempt to smooth over an awkward exchange. However, the more I promoted this alternate perspective, the more I realized how much better and more truthful it felt. I had never tallied the blessings that transpired in the years after the rape, but I was confident there were plenty.

As I puzzled with writing my impact statement, another thought demanded my attention. My experiences with dowsing, the firewalk, and affirmative prayers for the health of my daughter had convinced me that there was a connection between thoughts or focus and the outcome experienced. I began to wonder if I'd had some formative thoughts or feelings that might have aligned me with a trauma such as rape. This was a sensitive path to navigate. In my volunteer duties as a crisis advocate with our local rape crisis center, my work upheld one of their core beliefs: People who experience sexual violence are not to blame. Perpetrators of sexual violence are to blame.

Forgiveness

I didn't feel I was blaming myself as much as I was wanting to piece together what part I might have played in manifesting the rape and the massive transformation it had created. I knew this line of thought could be misconstrued as victim blaming. Still, it felt worthy of consideration.

I called my friend Sandi, director of education at our local rape crisis center. As a victim advocate, Sandi was thoughtful and discerning. Like me, she had a degree in chemistry, and I appreciated her logical way of thinking.

"Sandi, I know this may sound like victim blaming, but this is my experience, and I'd love your input. Do you think someone's thoughts or focus could align them with becoming victimized? Could their thoughts actually draw such a horrible experience to them? I mean, it was rape by a stranger. I didn't feel I could affect such happenings until I started thinking more about it."

Sandi listened patiently and then spoke. "I'd warn against faulting yourself for the rape," she said. I thought of my friend Martie, who'd scolded me for cycling alone on remote roads. His faultfinding had been hurtful and demeaning.

"No, I'm not seeing it as my fault," I explained. "I just feel I may have unconsciously aligned myself with this experience so I could learn something from it."

"You're entitled to couch it whatever way feels meaningful to you, Anne," Sandi replied. "Why do you think you might have aligned with this experience?"

It was a good question. I was curious about what had been in the heart and mind of a younger me. Looking closely at the positive outcomes of the rape would be like following breadcrumbs back to intentions I'd held as my twenty-six-year-old self. Perhaps one of the crumbs would help me remember.

"That's the piece I'm not yet clear on," I said. "If I believe our thoughts and feelings direct our experience, then I likely played a role in this happening. I'm curious if there's something I was seeking as a twenty-six-year-old that would have resulted in a traumatic event. My goal isn't to find out 'why I was raped,' so much as it is to create a story that works for me. If I can identify something I was focused on at that point in my life that led me down the gravel road and ultimately to where I am now, this deeper meaning will give me clarity to move forward. I'm imagining this information will direct my healing—and my life's work."

"Okay, now I understand better where you're coming from. The meaning you assign to your experience is important. If it helps you to think about it this way, by all means, adopt it. You're likely the only one who could answer what that focus was at age twenty-six."

I'd hoped Sandi would provide some insight, perhaps a story of someone with similar feelings about their trauma, but her response was disappointingly neutral. Still, it felt good to have a respected friend affirm my feelings, and I decided I'd not be deterred. I'd had enough validation of the influence of affirmative prayer that I sensed I might unearth something powerful by diving deeper into this question. Viewing the rape as a path to some useful outcome felt hopeful; it seemed the best way to reframe my story so that life supported me.

As spring approached, words for my statement began to flow as if they'd melted from some frozen place deep inside me. This was heartening, but with the defrosting of my emotion, I felt a heightened concern about appearing in court in just a few weeks. As I imagined being in the same room as my perpetrator, I realized I wasn't emotionally prepared. In my mind's eye, I saw us standing face-to-face and felt suddenly ill and unsteady. This was not the strength I'd envisioned.

I thought of my encounter with the angel, and how I'd feared its presence because I didn't understand it. To shift my perceptions, I had directed loving energy toward the visitor I feared. It was an illogical experiment, but as I whispered gentle words and prayers from my pillow, I had found myself more at ease with turning out the lights at night. With the calm of acceptance, I felt warmth reciprocated from the unseen being. Perhaps a similar practice would work for the perpetrator. As I thought about reframing my relationship with him, I was reminded of a dream I'd had over ten years earlier, when I was settling into Asheville.

It was a sleepy afternoon, almost two years after the rape. I was napping and dreamt of the rapist as a young boy. Dream recall (or even dreaming) was not common for me then, which is why the experience stands out. In the dream, I strangely experienced myself as the boy, and therefore I knew the rapist in a new way. Though I don't recall details of the dreamscape, I remember feeling his fear and discomfort in life, and I realized our shared humanness. I woke up in tears, knowing it best to let go of any anger I held toward him. We were both wounded; we had both felt fear and at times had acted out of that fear. I knew I'd want others to forgive me for whatever I suffered; wouldn't he want the same for himself? The dream led me to understand that my anger didn't help either of us.

After the dream, I wanted to feel forgiveness rather than anger toward the rapist. But I didn't know how to cultivate forgiveness. So I turned to logic. I rationalized that I'd spent only moments with this man—painful moments but moments nonetheless—and I didn't want to give him any more of my time or energy. It seemed reasonable to deny him this attention. However, every cell of my body held the trauma he'd caused. So forgiveness was not an instant transformation.

It didn't take me long to learn that my anger toward the perpetrator hurt *me* far more than it would ever affect him. For a couple years after the rape, burdensome thoughts and emotions had run marathons in my mind and body, most of them centered on the perpetrator. One spring morning in Manassas as I was driving to work, I became so agitated I was yelling obscenities at the rapist. I wouldn't have done that in my apartment where neighbors could hear, but my car was a safe haven. Unfortunately, my intensity was accompanied by increased pressure on the gas pedal, and I was pulled over and ticketed for driving fifty in a twenty-five-mile-an-hour zone. The inner torment was exhausting, but I was responsible for it. Allowing my mind to spin out of control inevitably led to my own suffering.

I felt entitled to my anger and upset, and rightly so. This man had changed my life as I'd known it; he had injured me in ways I couldn't put into words, and at that point there was little hope in his being identified and justice served. But my attachment to anger made me feel as if letting it go would create a void so immense I'd disappear into it.

It took some years and discipline to interrupt my emotional patterns. After the dream, I began by noticing my anxiety and reminding myself that I could choose peace. I practiced slowing my breathing and redirecting my energy toward soothing thoughts. After a few months, I was able to significantly reduce the time between noticing my upset and redirecting my attention. Each time I practiced suspending my bitter thoughts, I felt my connection with the rape begin to transform and my relationship to the rapist become less toxic and more temperate.

Though I'd heard about forgiveness throughout my life and practiced it in mundane life situations, I realized I didn't know its essential nature—especially in a situation where the core of myself had been brutally violated. I initially thought forgiveness was an act directed outward toward the man who raped me, but it didn't work that way. I couldn't simply decide to forgive him;

I couldn't force myself to feel neutral when I thought of him. I had to learn that forgiveness was a choice to lay down resentment and choose ease, whenever I was able. It was an act of love for myself. I wasn't going to excuse his wrongdoing or forget the crime, but I could hold compassion for myself. More broadly, by reminding myself that suffering was something I shared with the rapist, I could then hold some compassion for him. This was one path to finding windows of greater peace.

But windows open and close, and feeling forgiveness in one moment did not guarantee it in the next. I'd be feeling fine one minute and then become frustrated by breath that caught in my chest or angered by piercing pain in my hips. Tension would take hold in my shoulders and belly, my thoughts would sour and drift toward blame, and I'd have to redirect myself. It was some of my most intimate work, requiring me to be objective, look at my situation from new perspectives, reach for a touchstone such as my dream about the rapist, let go of my resistance, and become receptive to some other stance. To my amazement, in the moments I could manage this, I always discovered peace within reach.

My angst about the upcoming court appearance let me know there was another layer of work to be done. I desperately wanted to feel more at ease with myself and with the perpetrator. My short-term goal was to feel sturdy and relatively unruffled when I saw him in person. Long-term, I wanted the inner balance and freedom that I knew would come with transforming my angst.

In my search for a way to shift my emotions, I came across a blessing ritual from a dowsing workshop I'd attended years prior. The blessing creates balance and harmony where one has previously experienced division. This, along with forgiveness work, seemed a viable remedy as I worked on the impact statement. With the court date less than a month away, I began a daily practice of blessing the man who'd raped me and offering him forgiveness.

I woke early and sat on the meditation cushion in the middle of the living room floor, a tealight candle burning before me. I blessed myself, then blessed my perpetrator and added my own words of forgiveness.

"Creator, please bless me," I began. "Support the healing and the balance of my complete being . . ."

These blessings were far from a passive act; I would be appearing in court as a step toward healing myself and would not go in with half-hearted intention. As days passed, the thread of my connection with the rapist strengthened; I was soon referring to him by his first name.

"Creator, bless Terry. Support his healing and balance. In forgiveness of him and his violent acts, I release any anger or bitterness I hold now, and I invite in peace and acceptance for myself and for him. Please help him to feel the power of forgiveness."

I viewed my connection with Terry as I had in my dream. Part of him was me; part of me was him. We shared struggle in our lives—both wounded, both in need of healing. Prayer was a powerful balm.

I found myself warming to the thought of standing in my power before him. As springtime prompted new growth, I felt as though some part of me had also sprouted; buds of possibility and hope for new beginnings became part of my inner terrain.

Meanwhile, my writing was graced with a fresh sense of clarity. I soon produced a statement that felt true and complete. I was becoming a new person because of it. I hadn't discounted or left behind the turmoil I'd experienced but voiced how I'd learned and grown in the aftermath of trauma. Writing my victim statement stretched me to look more holistically at the experience, to articulate the blessings born of adversity, and to embrace what I'd learned as worthy of gratitude. Presenting my statement in person to the court, my family, my friends, and the perpetrator would be the next step in the process. All around, this opportunity seemed to be shaping me into a vessel that could hold greater strength.

15

Presence

After devoting three months to writing a statement for an
April court date, I was informed the hearing would be
postponed until November. The news deflated me. With the
time and energy I'd invested in gaining clarity on my statement
and building myself up for a court appearance, I simply wanted
to get it over with.

In retrospect, however, the delay was a good thing. I continued my blessings of Terry but still felt edgy about the upcoming
encounter. I clearly had more inner work to do if I wanted to
be grounded in November, though I wasn't sure what this work
would look or feel like. I'd spent years feeling disconnected from
my body; often I felt I was floating somewhere above my experience. Intent on being fully present in the courtroom, I focused
my prayers on that as my outcome.

I wasn't disappointed. In early October, George, a friend's
husband whom I didn't know well, called me out of the blue.

"I'm taking a weekly guided meditation class," he said, "and
I've had a repeated vision that I think you should know about."
Curious, I listened.

"In these visions, I saw you with someone I know. His name is Dr. Andersen. He's an osteopath in Fletcher. I have a sense he may be able to help you in some way."

I didn't hesitate. George gave me Dr. Andersen's number; I dialed his office and scheduled an appointment for the next week. I was uncertain how to approach my meeting with Dr. Andersen. It seemed silly to ask a doctor I'd just met if he could help me be more present, but in my heart something was calling me in this direction. I did my best to convince myself I wasn't wasting time by following this lead. *He's an osteopath. He'll likely be able to unlock the uncomfortable places in my body, and hopefully he'll answer my prayers for presence.*

Dr. Andersen lived and worked not far from my home. His office was unusually located on the lower level of a building that housed a small diner. The reception room, small and sparsely decorated, was nonetheless comfortable. Its coffee table featured a large hand-carved wooden bear standing on its hind legs. Perhaps it was the bear's imposing stance or that it was made of solid wood and towered above any other structure in the room, including the lamp on the side table, but whatever it was, the bear seemed to exude an energy far larger than the tiny room could hold. As I waited, I could hear the bustle of waitresses serving lunch upstairs.

Soon Dr. Andersen appeared, filling the doorway with his presence like the bear sculpture filled the reception room. He motioned me back to his office, a windowless room warmly lit with ceiling lights and adorned with two large-cushioned chairs upholstered in tasteful earth tones. We sat in the chairs facing one another and talked about my reason for being there. I began slowly, and with his questioning, I'd soon shared the whole story: the rape, the DNA match, George's vision, and my search for presence and wholeness. Dr. Andersen was kind and somehow mysterious. His confident demeanor gave me the sense that he knew things about me that I myself wasn't aware of. This was a little unsettling, but I remained curious.

Once he was clear about what I needed, he asked me to hop on the examining table so he could work on my imbalances. As I lay on my back, Dr. Andersen placed one hand under my neck and one at the base of my spine. I could feel an immense healing power in his hands, which with stubby, somewhat bent fingers, looked strangely similar to a bear's claws. His two hands seemed to be speaking a language of energy, impulses darting from one end of my spine to the other. Unlike the sudden force of a chiropractic adjustment, his manipulation was accomplished through a combination of gentle pressure and stretching. Within moments, I felt my alignment shift and change, and I adjusted my body accordingly on the table. I was amazed how much better I felt when I stood up.

"You'll feel a bit different now. I moved some things around," he said casually.

"Thanks," I replied. And I meant it. My pelvis felt solid and level, my spine more supple, and my movement more fluid. His adjustment had clearly established a new balance for my body.

"I know you're wanting to be fully present in the courtroom," he said. "You need to meet Will Rockingbear." He reached for a notepad on a side table and began to write. "He's a Cherokee elder who lives up in Yancey County. Go to him and request a soul retrieval." He handed me the slip of paper on which he'd scribbled Rockingbear's name and phone number.

By that point I'd experienced numerous alternative healing modalities—massage and meditation, acupuncture and qigong, homeopathy, and essential oils. But I'd never sat with a Native American elder.

"Could you describe soul retrieval?" I asked.

"Well," Dr. Andersen began, "Rockingbear's a Cherokee medicine man, a shaman. He interacts directly with the spirit world to address aspects of illness or imbalance. A soul retrieval is a ceremony performed to bring back lost parts of the soul."

"How might I have misplaced parts of my soul?"

"It's really self-preservation. It's believed that when we suffer emotional or physical trauma, part of our soul leaves the body in order to survive the experience. So, you end up having less of your life force or vitality available to you."

Whoa. I suddenly had lots of questions. "But where does the soul go?"

"That's a good question. In psychology, the loss would likely be called disassociation, but psychologists don't talk about what parts of the soul disassociate and where these parts go. A shaman would probably say that a piece of the soul leaves the body and goes into non-ordinary reality, where it waits until someone intervenes in the spirit world and facilitates its return."

"So what makes you think parts of my soul are gone?"

"The rape, the trauma. Often, someone who's experienced soul loss doesn't feel fully in her body or engaged in life. I'm pretty certain you'll benefit from this ceremony."

Though it sounded like something from a science fiction novel, I felt strongly I was being led, so I followed. When I arrived home that afternoon, I sat on my porch in the autumn sun and gave Rockingbear a call.

It was a short conversation in which I explained the situation. "I want to be completely present when I enter the courtroom next month. Dr. Andersen felt a soul retrieval would be in order."

"I can go look for you," Rockingbear said, his words slow and thoughtful. "I'll simply retrieve any parts of your soul that have separated themselves."

The word "simply" struck me as funny. My cynicism typically lurked backstage as I stepped into new healing scenarios. At that point I'd spent fourteen years trying to heal myself. His certainty made me wonder if I'd been wasting my time on efforts that didn't address the real problem. It didn't seem a simple task to me, but this was new territory, and I wanted to remain open to the possibility that there were people who could "simply" put your soul back together again.

"Okay," I replied. "I appreciate your help with this."

"You've requested ceremony," Rockingbear continued with deliberateness. "Ceremony begins with the asking. I encourage you to pay attention to who comes into your experience and to what's happening around you this next week before you come see me." The purposeful way he spoke caused me to pay close attention to his words; I hadn't considered that my life might begin to shift with the request. We set a day and time to meet, and he gave me directions to his home.

Earth Green Medicine Lodge, Rockingbear's home and place of work, was about an hour's drive north of Asheville. It was situated atop a mountain at the end of a long, steep gravel road scattered with pits and pockets that required close attention on my tortoise-like ascent. I arrived at the lodge on a bright windy afternoon and parked outside the garage door, where a rock wall marked the entrance to a sunny backyard garden. A small heart-shaped stone was prominently displayed in the wall's central rock cavity.

The walk to the front door was densely skirted with large green hostas and hardwood trees that provided ample shade from the southern sun. I walked up the three steps to the deck and tentatively called out at the screen door. I felt someone was sitting just inside.

"Aho," I heard. "Come in." I entered, my eyes adjusting to the dim interior light. Rockingbear was seated in a padded leather chair on the far side of a table. I walked around to greet him.

"Have a seat," he said, motioning to the chair in front of him.

Will Rockingbear was seventy-something, of moderate stature with a thinning frame. His head was hairless, speckled with a few wrinkles and age spots, his face highlighted by a thick white mustache that flowed around the corners of his mouth and tapered downward, encircling his chin.

"This is for you," I said hesitantly as I handed him a bundle of tobacco wrapped in red felt. Directed by Dr. Andersen, I'd brought this offering. It was, I learned, proper etiquette in Native circles to gift an elder tobacco wrapped in red cloth when requesting ceremony. Tobacco is one of the sacred medicines of the Cherokee; it's used to bind a contract and to show honor and respect for the gift that's requested. I included a card with a monetary gift.

"Thank you," Rockingbear said, pulling the bundle close to his heart and reaching his other hand down to touch the floor. This gesture, I later learned, affirms connection to all life and expresses gratitude to the earth for her abundant provision. A large orange cat peered from behind Rockingbear's chair and disappeared.

"Tell me what you come here for," Rockingbear said.

A little unsure of myself, I repeated what I'd shared in our phone conversation. "I feel you can help me be more present in the upcoming court hearing I'm attending. I haven't felt fully myself in a number of years. I don't know or understand your work but am following what feels like the next best step, and Dr. Andersen directed me this way."

My eyes had adjusted to the lighting, and I peered around the room. A woman was puttering in the kitchen behind me. I hadn't noticed her until that moment. She had long white hair, powerful but gentle eyes, and a broad smile.

"This is my partner, Zoe," Rockingbear said, motioning her to come closer. "She'll be drumming for our ceremony today."

"Nice to meet you," I said, lifting myself from the chair to greet her.

She took my hand and smiled. "Hello. Welcome." Then she turned back to the kitchen, shuffling papers on the counter in front of her.

"How long have you felt this lack of presence?" Rockingbear asked. "Can you remember when it began?"

Recalling how I'd drifted out of my body when I was assaulted and witnessed much of the event from somewhere above the situation, I said, "Well, I suspect there was some separation the day I was raped." I felt a little hesitant and cleared my throat. Rockingbear was, after all, a total stranger to me. But somehow I trusted him. "That was fourteen years ago."

"This disconnectedness is often felt by those who've lost part of their soul," he explained. "We won't know until we go look."

A second cat appeared, dark gray with black stripes. It retreated through the double glass doors behind Rockingbear and stood motionless mid-room, then skirted a corner into a neighboring hallway and disappeared. I began noticing more of my surroundings—some gemstones, a bundle of feathers, and several books were scattered across the nearby table; a large drum hung on the wall. I turned my attention back to Rockingbear.

"There are some times when we find cords or connections with people that are causing a drain in energy. If we find these, do I have your permission to cut them?"

I wondered what he meant by "cut," but with an impatient desire to move on to the business of retrieving my soul, I simply said, "Yes. That sounds like it'd be helpful."

"And should we find that your soul has separated, do you

give me permission to bring back the parts in order to restore wholeness?"

I knew I could answer that with confidence. "Yes, absolutely."

"You may be asked to make some agreements. It will be your choice," he explained.

"Okay." I didn't understand what I was agreeing to, but I felt grounded by Rockingbear's clarity and attentiveness to detail.

Rockingbear invited me and Zoe into the healing room. The room faced south, and sun poured in through the sliding glass door. The light seemed blinding. Two Mexican blankets had been spread on the floor atop a bear hide. I was directed to a shell containing sage and a lighter. Rockingbear asked me to light the sage, and once it was smoldering, Zoe took the shell and brushed it down the front of my body and up my back, allowing the smoke to clear my energy in preparation for ceremony.

Zoe picked up her drum and drumstick from a side table and gently ran her hand around the rim of the drum several times. Her soft caress of the drum's hide seemed executed with loving purpose. It was as if this light brushing woke the drum from a slumber. Its whispered breath filled the space, and I felt suddenly warmed from within. I was asked to lie on one of the blankets while Rockingbear stretched out just beside me on the other. We both placed bandanas over our eyes, and I lay still, wondering what would happen next.

"It's best if you don't do anything except make space inside for the lost pieces to return," Rockingbear said. "You can use your breath for this."

Zoe drummed while Rockingbear journeyed to inquire about my soul. I lost track of time during the ceremony; my mind drifted, and it's possible I slept. At some point, I was aware the drumming had stopped and I awakened (or simply became more conscious of where I was). Something felt distinctly differ-ent, but perhaps it was my imagination.

"Welcome," Rockingbear said softly. "Uncover your eyes and go take a look in the mirror. I think you'll see some changes."

I placed the bandana on the floor beside me, slowly moved my body to standing, and walked over to the large mirror on the wall. If something had visibly changed, I couldn't see it; but inside, I felt different. I was aware of an internal murmur, a rest-lessness that wanted soothing but felt just out of reach. I sensed something had come unhinged and needed securing.

Rockingbear invited me to sit with him as he shared what he'd experienced. Three soul pieces wished to be present with me. Surprisingly, none of them seemed directly related to the rape. If they were to stick around, I'd need to make agreements with them. These were not agreements like those you make with your husband about picking up the bread or milk at the grocery. These were long-term commitments to some lost part of me, and Rockingbear emphasized that they'd need to be upheld.

"What are the soul pieces telling you?" he asked.

I was perplexed. *How would a soul piece tell me something?*

"I . . . I don't know."

"Yes, you do. Pay attention and trust yourself. Go in and ask them."

I closed my eyes and focused on the first soul piece we had discussed. I posed a question in my head that felt obvious and direct. *What do you have to tell me?* I inquired awkwardly, not expecting any answers. I paused, my mind working hard to cre-ate something itself, so as not to appear lacking answers, but it didn't seem to work. *Perhaps I need to try harder.*

Rockingbear, obviously sensing my discomfort, began to guide me with questions. He gave me a little information about the first soul piece—when it had separated, under what circumstances—and then asked me what it wanted from me. With his help, I began tuning into these pieces and getting clear answers. I didn't share this with Rockingbear; it felt intimate, something I wanted to keep to myself. When I got stuck, Rockingbear asked just the right question for me to refocus and get the information I needed. Sometimes I'd answer his questions directly; other times, we'd share a few words and he would affirm what I felt. I continued, addressing each piece separately, gathering the details needed to assure I could meet its needs and that it would remain with me from here on out. It was intimate work, as I recalled memories of people and places and feelings from childhood in Barnesville, from the years following my move to Oxford, and from life in Manassas. How could I have overlooked the parts that had gone missing? I sensed that I'd been careless not to notice and felt sorrow about being remiss, about lost opportunities, and about people who'd once touched and then wounded my heart. Tears streamed quietly down my face.

Rockingbear asked me to speak aloud my commitments to the lost parts of my soul. As words flowed from my lips, I sensed the sacredness of what was occurring. This act was shifting something much larger than just me. There was a distinct interconnectedness between me and the people and situations that had just been brought to my awareness, and I understood that my commitments were mending relations with myself and with them. I was struck by the power of this work, and by the importance of honoring the agreements I'd just made. These moments would surely impact me for years to come; my mind was already reeling with what the agreements might require of me. If I desired to keep these soul pieces intact, I was obligated from that moment forward to listen more intently to their voices and to act on their behalf.

"It's important not to speak to others about this work for at least four days and nights or for as long as feels comfortable to you," Rockingbear said. "Your silence maintains the sacredness of what's occurred. It keeps the energy close and potent. This is how you'll want it to be as you work with these parts of yourself."

I considered his words and felt the truth in them. I thanked him for his help, and though I had many questions, I wanted to honor his time. Before leaving, I asked Rockingbear if there was a way I could learn more from him. He invited me to come sit with him in his weekly Wednesday night circle.

I followed a different route home that day by way of the Blue Ridge Parkway. I needed time and wanted to be surrounded by beauty. I was, according to Rockingbear, a new person. Though I didn't understand the significance of this, I felt markedly changed. My restlessness had transformed into stillness. I noticed it in the slowness of my breath, in my relaxed body, and in my desire to simply be present and not rush on to the next thing. I stopped at a scenic overlook where I sat on a hillside, my back against a large oak to shelter me from the wind. There I opened my journal and began recording my thoughts about what had just transpired. I found myself challenged to describe what was real. The ceremony, after all, seemed simple and metaphoric, yet it held profound personal meaning and a transformative power. As I sat, pen in hand, I felt my mind relax. My attention drifted away from the journal to the stunning colors of the fall mountains, to the earth that supported me, and to my precious easy breathing. I relinquished my need to understand, drew in a breath that seemed to expand the depth of my heart, and felt unusually content to appreciate the moment.

16

Statement

Detective Newsome contacted me again in mid-October, confirming our November court date. "The *Washington Post* has contacted me several times," he said. "They're interested in your story. I'll give you the reporter's contact information, and you can decide what you'd like to do."

I'd gained confidence and clarity preparing my impact statement and thought my story could support others who'd experienced trauma. If the reporter could write a piece that focused on hope and healing, it was worth investing my time and energy in that direction. I also felt an interview could be an opportunity to explore things more deeply myself.

Ian Shapira, the *Post* reporter, arrived in Asheville in early November and spent a day and a half with me. He was intent on understanding the rape and subsequent years of healing from my perspective: what I remembered from that day, how I had navigated the months following, what had transpired in the fourteen years between the rape and Newsome's phone call, and the impact the event had had on my life. We sat together for several extended periods—in my living room, on the front

119

porch—discussing details and digging deep. Occasionally he included Tom in the process, asking him to share his version of various events. Ian held sincere interest in my story, and his stream of inquiries was thoughtful, his communication warm and sensitive. Many years later, he would tell me how grateful he was that I was going public with my story and how nervous he had been to be responsible for covering it. I was comfortable with his questioning. What I didn't anticipate was how exhausted I would become digging into the past, remembering places and people, and feeling the emotions again.

When Ian departed, I didn't take time to tend to the emotions that had surfaced during his inquiry. Instead, I focused on connecting with old friends and acquaintances who had come up in conversation and who had supported me in the aftermath of the rape. I made phone calls and sent e-mails to these supporters in hopes I could see them when I visited Manassas in November. Taking these actions kept me seemingly in control of my feelings.

Ian's article made the front page of the *Washington Post* on Tuesday, November 16, 2004. That day, my phone didn't stop ringing as the nation's top media networks tried to reach me to do their own TV or radio spot. I let it ring while e-mails flowed in from friends and strangers who'd found my e-mail address attached to online articles I'd written for a local women's magazine. I wasn't inclined to follow up with requests for interviews; my focus was on Friday of that week, when I would appear in court and read my statement.

But in the midst of preparing to travel to Manassas, one media request came to the forefront. Diane Sawyer of ABC's *Good Morning America* wanted to speak with me. After several failed attempts to contact me directly, she had an ABC representative drive two hours from Charlotte to my home in Asheville to invite me to be interviewed by Ms. Sawyer. I was doing my best to lie low, but with respect for Sawyer and her journalistic achievements, I invited the representative into my home. Having driven all that way, I expected the woman to be pushy. Another reporter had shown up unannounced the day prior and, once she was at my door, was relentless in pursuit of an interview. To the contrary, the woman from ABC was patient and attentive to my concerns. She explained what an interview on *Good Morning America* would look like and assured me Sawyer would work closely with me to make such an interview a win for all concerned. I decided to be interviewed if Sawyer could assure me the interview would present a message of hope. The representative confirmed my request and e-mailed me that evening to let me know Ms. Sawyer would call me the day before Thanksgiving to discuss the interview.

Before then, however, my attention would be on my court appearance. I had continued my blessing and forgiveness practice, a daily action that softened my tension and opened me to the possibility I could face Terry feeling a sense of confidence and peace. As well, I asked my practitioner friends to do affirmative prayer for me, and I was, to my amazement, feeling confident as I anticipated the journey north and the reading of my statement.

Our family planned to drive to Manassas, stopping briefly to visit my parents on the way. Tom's brother, who lived in Maryland, would care for Joseph while Tom watched one-year-old Liza at the courthouse. I'd contacted friends in Manassas, several of whom planned to appear at the court proceedings in support. Things seemed to be falling into place with an ease and flow that was reassuring. This was not something I took for granted. For most of the last fourteen years, I'd felt I was living precariously, perched on the edge of emotional and physical instability.

I'd worked diligently to secure my footing in life, often with a faltering sense of success. But as I prepared for the trip, I sensed I was beginning to walk on solid, level ground.

In the hotel room in Manassas the morning of the hearing, I pulled my skirt and blouse from my suitcase. My MS ride number, a little bent and tattered, was safety-pinned at its corners to the back of my blouse, which I'd carefully folded into the suitcase. I slid the blouse over my head and adjusted the number on my back, then slipped on my navy suit jacket. My cycling friends called me "five-eleven." It would be a comfort to wear that number when I stepped into the courtroom. I was surprised to have found it tucked in a box of scrapbook items in our basement. It reminded me of days of strength, of freedom and wholeness; I was reclaiming these qualities by showing up at the hearing.

The November day was overcast and a tad chilly. It had rained the night before, and roads were still damp. Tom and I drove from our hotel to the Prince William County Courthouse and parked. I exited the car slowly, and we double-checked the lock on my bike, which hung from the back rack on our car. I looked forward to the possibility of getting out for a ride later in the day.

Crowds of reporters had already gathered at the building's entrance. I hadn't anticipated that, but with the *Post* article having appeared at the start of the week, I wasn't surprised. I took a deep breath as I walked toward the building, my red leather binder under my arm, my statement folded inside. Tom walked beside me carrying Liza in his arms; she had celebrated her first birthday in October and was alert and curious in these new surroundings. As we approached the door, reporters, notebooks in hand, streamed toward me. Microphones were pushed to my face.

"Ms. Heck, what are you feeling about being asked to appear in court?"

"What were your thoughts when you first heard from the detective?"

I felt uneasy walking through the barrage of questions. I did my best to hasten through the crowd, putting my hand up to fend off engagement and minimize eye contact.

A woman in a light blue raincoat stepped toward me with a small mic in hand. "Ms. Heck, may we have a statement? It'll only take a moment."

"I'll be offering my statement in the courtroom," I said, hoping others wouldn't push in any closer. I felt grateful to reach the courthouse door.

A friendly woman named Tammy met us as we stepped into the building. She ushered us down the hall, through a mahogany doorway, and into an attractive study furnished with leather-bound chairs and law books.

"Please make yourself comfortable. I'll come get you when we're about to get started. Would you like some tea?" Tammy asked.

"No, thank you. I'm fine," I replied.

To Tom she said, "I'll be happy to take care of your daughter if you'd like to be in the courtroom with Anne. Come this way, and I'll show you how all that will work."

Tom, Liza, and Tammy left, closing the door behind them. I was relieved to have a quiet space to gather myself. As much as I appreciated the presence of family, Liza's squirminess distracted me at a time when I wanted to stay balanced and clear. I was grateful to Tom for seeing to the children's needs.

I looked out the window where I could just see the edge of the crowd of reporters. Then I paced the carpet, stretched my arms over my head, practiced deep breathing, and did my best to ground myself in this unfamiliar place. *You're gonna be just fine*, I told myself. *It's all good.*

A Fierce Belief in Miracles

I hadn't set foot in Manassas since I'd moved away thirteen years earlier; I hadn't wanted to. I'd dedicated those years to rebuilding my confidence and to healing my body. And there was still work to be done. That day, November 19, 2004, Prince William County Circuit Court requested my presence and my statement. It had come about, clearly, as a result of my earnest prayer for strength, and I understood—to a degree—the importance of being fully present and speaking my truth.

The wait seemed uncomfortably long; I did my best to stay focused on my breath. I could feel emotion repeatedly rising up to my chest, sometimes to my throat. When it came up too far for me to easily hold it down, I'd breathe and begin focusing on my feet—feeling my toes in my shoes, the soles of my feet solidly connected to the floor. Eventually the door opened, and a court assistant escorted me down long well lit hallways to the courtroom. I was directed to the front row of wooden benches where Tom was already seated. As I sat beside him, I briefly sighed, relieved that the court session would soon be underway.

The courtroom walls were paneled in a light oak wood that matched the judge's bench, the tables, and the jury box. The carpet was a bright ocean blue, which seemed to lighten the space, but for a brief moment my mind fixed on how suitable it would feel had it been scarlet red. I recalled the rapist's red car that had disappeared from sight that morning as I stood in shock on the edge of the forest.

Tom and I were seated in the front row of the spectator section, behind several chairs where, I soon realized, sat Terry McDonald. He was dressed in a white prison uniform, an officer and a public defender seated on either side of him. Though I could only see the side of his face, I couldn't say I recognized him. Seeing him felt anticlimactic. Little, if any, emotion surfaced. *If he turned to face me, if I could see his eyes, would I feel differently?* I wondered. *Would I feel fear? Would I feel relief?*

The room was brought to order. The judge made some opening remarks, then asked me to come forward to make my statement. I stood and was escorted by an officer to the left front of the courtroom where I was directed to sit behind a wooden bench. I straightened my papers on the small desk in front of me, gave attention to relaxing the tension in my shoulders, and peered into the court audience. Terry was sitting in the front row, directly across from me, his head bowed. I looked beyond him, my eyes meeting Tom's, and I reminded myself to breathe.

There were other friendly faces scattered among the onlookers. Several colleagues from the school where I used to teach were seated toward the front, their spouses beside them. And Ted, my cycling buddy from years ago, was there. I knew he would appreciate the number I'd pinned to my back. A breath. My chest felt tight, and emotions began to bubble up in my throat. Though I didn't make eye contact, I sensed Terry looking my way. I looked beyond him to Tom and to my many supporters. Another breath. There were other spectators present—reporters scribbling notes and drawing images, and people I didn't know. I later learned there were attendees who came to sit in support after reading the *Post* article.

Still seated behind the bench, I was unsure when to begin.

"Anytime you're ready," the judge said as he looked my way.

Remaining seated, I peered down at my statement and began reading:

> *I was raped in July of 1990. It was a beautiful summer day, and I was enjoying a road trip on my bicycle exploring back roads. I loved the freedom I felt on two wheels with the sun*

on my back. What a stark contrast this incident was to my intention for that day.

I felt tears warming my eyes, and I glanced up, breathing in the support of my friends and my husband.

As one can expect, this crime has had a huge impact on my life. Without this experience, I feel I would have missed out on much of the richness available to me. While I don't believe this richness need come only when faced with adversity, I do believe this horrific event provided a background of contrast that created a more vivid palette for my life. At age forty, and fourteen years after this event, I can honestly say that I'm grateful for the growth this path has provided me.

While I do not condone Mr. McDonald's act, and feel he should receive his just sentence, I've come to accept this as a chapter of my life that has provided me with the potential for my personal healing and development.

There are many facets of this growth that I believe serve witness to the impact this rape has had on my life, and I'd like to share a few of those:

The day I was raped, I learned about friendship and kindness when a stranger picked me up along that dusty road and took me crumpled and terror-stricken to the closest paramedic unit. A rather new acquaintance made calls to dentists for me.

Again, I glanced up, catching Ted's eyes and nodding a thank-you. Tears rose to my eyes. *Breathe.*

I had two teeth that were knocked out of place, and a kind doctor agreed to stay late to help me. Unfortunately, the teeth were irreparable, the roots damaged. I would eventually have to have root canals and other reparative work done to them.

Statement

I learned about letting go as I had my favorite blue biking shorts and shirt, stained with blood, bagged by police, and taken away for evidence.

I grew into new ways of viewing my freedom as I had my trusty touring bike covered in black fingerprint dust returned to my apartment. It sat untouched for weeks.

I remember with disgust the volunteer at the hospital who came into my room to read scripture and tell me I could be forgiven for my sins. I experienced what it felt like to be shunned at the health center when I went in for a pregnancy test and shared that I had been raped. I quickly learned to trust my own knowing that I had done nothing wrong.

I paused, allowing my emotions to settle a bit. My next words felt challenging. Perhaps it was best my parents weren't in the courtroom.

A dear friend of mine drove to see me the day after the rape; he loaded me in his car and drove me to my parents' home. My parents were mostly silent, unable themselves to process the emotion of what had happened. I learned that those who love you often have the hardest time expressing their hurt to you.

I wiped my nose and paused, my left hand touching my chest lightly, a gentle reminder to bring my focus back to my breath, to become present with my body.

At the beginning, I remember with some fuzziness passing many days in deep fear, jumping at the smallest sounds, panicking at daybreak, dizzy from my lack of breath, unable to face crowds or put myself in the presence of strangers. I learned to give credence to my intuition and listen to my body.

Months passed, and I had the opportunity to participate in group and personal counseling, both of which I abhorred, as it was extremely challenging to get to the emotion of my experience when that emotion was mostly trapped in my body. I learned patience with the process and had the opportunity to look closer at my own character.

I woke many nights with a vivid picture of the perpetrator in my head and often drew pictures of him hoping that putting it on paper would somehow purge my body of my relentless fearful thoughts and feelings. This taught me to let my emotions flow through me.

I learned about patience and trust as I waited ten days to receive the results of my HIV test.

I experienced my lack of readiness for learning self-defense when I broke into uncontrolled tears at my first class; I learned how to be kind to myself.

After several more months, I did complete a self-defense class that allowed me to release lots of the emotion I had packed in my body. My women colleagues where I taught high school all came to support me at my graduation.

I gazed out to the attendees and nodded in gratitude to the women who sat in support of me—the same women who witnessed my graduation years ago.

I learned how deeply all women are affected by acts of rape and abuse, and I learned wherever women come together, there is intense power that can be created.

A year after my rape, I left Manassas, hoping to leave my intense emotions behind and find a more peaceful environment in which to heal. Initially panic set in, and I gradually learned how to build a support system for myself. I had the good opportunity to find a wonderful group of supporters at a local rape crisis center, whom I called on periodically when my body was remembering the trauma and my mind didn't know how to process it.

After much more counseling and lots of tears, I undertook training as an advocate at the rape crisis center and also served on their speaker's bureau. There I learned how very many women shared my horror, and I learned how to respond appropriately to those who were healing as well as those who had never experienced rape.

Within a couple of years, I had received training in women's self-defense from a number of programs and began teaching assertiveness training to young women. I had great passion for the topic and quit my teaching position at a local high school to devote my time fully to this endeavor. Through this I gained confidence and strength and a deep admiration for women.

Again, I paused to connect with my breath and my body. I suddenly realized how fatigued I felt, but knew I was nearly complete. I glanced over at Tom; this helped me gather strength to continue.

As time has passed, I have thought about that horrid day less and less. What has remained is a fairly constant and often severe pain in my pelvis and hips. This pain began the year following the rape and has certainly been my most constant reminder that there is emotion that has not been released— it's my body's reminder that I still have some growing to do.

I have met with all types of medical, psychological, and alternative health professionals over the years, always hoping to find the path that would relieve my pain. I've gone through too many months of feeling tired and frustrated from this drain in energy, and weeks of being unable to walk.

I have two young children now who are vibrant with life's energy, and I long to experience my own peak health and fully enjoy my time with them. Indeed, I'm ready for that piece of growth that provides me my freedom.

The time for that growth is now, and my intent for participating in this sentencing is to close this chapter of my life, to release whatever negative emotion I'm still holding in my body, and to feel the freedom and joy that I so clearly had that morning fourteen years ago when I left home to enjoy a day of biking.

Some people tell me I'm courageous for appearing in court. I believe I'm blessed to have the opportunity to experience this part of my healing process. This event is for me a symbolic statement of hope, justice, and my own personal freedom.

Thank you.

My cheeks were moist with tears, my one tissue pressed firmly in my palm. An officer motioned for me to return to my seat. My lungs took in a deep breath as I sat next to Tom; I welcomed his arm on my shoulder. The judge then addressed Terry.

"Does the defendant wish to make a statement?"

Terry rose and, to my surprise, turned to face me. We were barely six feet from one another, separated only by a row of chairs. He looked directly into my eyes. His body was bulky, his face drawn. His thinning hair and bare forehead seemed to bring my attention to the parts of his face that I could remember, but barely—the tight lips, small nose, and beady, close-set eyes. His eyes had looked so desperate that day; today they looked softer, tired. I returned his gaze, neither fearful nor relieved, but feeling mysteriously connected with this stranger and with the moment.

"Ms. Anne," he addressed me. He paused and then continued. "I'm very sorry for what I did that day. There's not enough I can say to show that I'm sorry. You give me the courage to get counseling. I'm a victim of something myself. I wish I could change. I hope you can accept my apology." He looked directly into my eyes and lowered his voice so that it was only audible to those seated close. "Thank you for forgiving me," he added, his eyes intense and purposeful.

He knew. My prayers of forgiveness—he knew.

I felt a lump in my throat, my eyes burning with tears. Silently, I placed my palms together before my chest and nodded affirmingly to him, feeling deep gratitude and reverence for the connection and acknowledgment that had just transpired.

Then Terry turned to face the judge. "Your honor, I have an illness that I can't control. It would be best to lock me up until a cure is found."

The judge replied, "It's very easy for me to conclude you should be incarcerated for the rest of your life. You said so yourself."

Terry received two life sentences that day. He would return to West Virginia, where he was serving time for another crime. Years later he would be transferred to the Virginia prison system to serve time for his crimes against me.

I left the courtroom with Tom by my side. Tammy was waiting with Liza in her arms and directed us to exit through the back of the building to avoid reporters. She had a vehicle waiting there to drive us to our car.

Liza reached out to Tom, who lifted her up on his shoulder. My female colleagues crowded around with hugs of support. We all made plans to meet at a local diner down the street and visit. Ted walked up, smiled, and placed his arm around my shoulder. I gave him a big hug. Then I remembered the ride number, removed my navy jacket, and stepped out in front of my crowd of supporters, my back to them.

"Five-eleven! You go girl!" Ted shouted. We laughed as I threw my arms into the air, victorious.

PART TWO

17

Anger

For days following the court appearance, Terry's whispered "Thank you for forgiving me" replayed in my mind. Having my statement witnessed by friends, family, and the court provided me with satisfaction and a degree of confidence. But the most dramatic shift happened when Terry softly yet fully acknowledged me. My silent inner work had reached him.

That Terry's acknowledgment echoed the words of my prayer is something I could have dismissed as coincidence. Had it happened a few years prior, I might have done so. But by the court date, I'd used blessings and intentions for over a year and witnessed outcomes that seemed undeniably linked to my prayers. The courtroom encounter inspired the same feelings I held many mornings, sitting openhearted in my living room offering forgiveness to Terry. I recognized the physical sensation first—a gentle warmth rising from my belly to my heart as Terry turned to address me; it was an unexpected sensation in the courtroom setting—a reminder to pay attention to what was happening. While Terry's words amazingly matched those of my blessings, what impacted me most was the peace and harmony

I felt in our exchange. It was as if my angel—or perhaps many angels—had dropped down into the space between Terry and me, and whispered to my guarded heart: "Remain open and pay attention." I was humbled by the sacredness of the moment; its effects continued to pulse through my being that afternoon and in the days that followed. Openhearted blessings and forgiveness were powerful agents, the magnitude of which penetrated any resistance Terry held. This knowing strengthened me.

At a scheduled time the day before Thanksgiving, my phone rang, and I exchanged niceties with Diane Sawyer. We spoke of family and crowds at our homes for the holiday. I shared my desire that any coverage of my story hold a positive focus so that others might find hope through hearing it. She agreed, and we scheduled my live appearance on *Good Morning America* to take place the following Monday, November 29.

In two weeks' time, my story had been printed in the *Washington Post*, I'd traveled to Manassas to face my perpetrator in the courtroom, and I would fly to New York City to appear on national television. It was a dizzying amount of activity that began to feel both physically and emotionally draining.

As I was still nursing Liza, we traveled as a family to New York. Arriving Sunday afternoon, we were greeted at the airport by a limousine driver. He loaded our bags into his car and drove us into the heart of the city, delivering us to a hotel just doors from the ABC studio, our room overlooking Times Square.

Monday morning we rose early and ate a quick breakfast before walking over to the studio. My stomach felt tight as I signed in at reception, but I had little time to consider my emotions as I was whisked away from Tom and the children and led to a small room where I was introduced to a young makeup artist with ginger hair and dark eyes. She sat me in a leather chair in front of a Hollywood-style makeup mirror outlined by bright golf-ball lights and adorned me with thick eyelashes and satiny maroon lipstick. There wasn't much that could be done with my hair, which I kept extra short to prevent helmet head after cycling. Over Thanksgiving I had driven to the nearest shopping mall and found some black dress slacks, a black crew sweater, and a tasteful red blazer with black highlights. Red felt fitting for the day's appearance.

In the greenroom, I sat on a couch with Liza in my lap as Tom entertained her with a hand puppet. Joseph, now five years old, sat beside me watching the news feed on the screen in the corner of the room. I wasn't sure how he'd be affected watching the episode about me, and I felt concern for him. I hadn't shielded him from my story; in our family conversations, we referred to the perpetrator as the "not-nice man," and Joseph knew I'd been hurt by him. Holding my daughter, I began to feel prickles of anxiety or excitement—or both—about appearing on national television; my body felt chilled and shaky. I wanted to be clear and purposeful in providing hope for viewers and was concerned I might not think quickly and clearly enough to offer suitable response. Luckily, my wait was short-lived. During a commercial break, I was led into the recording studio. Though the stage was surrounded on one side by cameras, the rest of the space was like a comfortable living room. Bookshelves lined one wall; a Christmas tree lit up a corner. A Persian rug covered the center of the dark cherry flooring, and two beige armchairs sat in the middle of the space facing one another.

Diane Sawyer approached and greeted me. She was dressed in a gray cardigan and black pants, a string of pearls around her neck. The lights in the studio suddenly seemed excessively bright, and I felt my face flush as she welcomed me to her studio living room. We sat facing each other in the beige chairs as the cameraman counted "five, four, three . . ." to the end of the commercial break. Sawyer set the scene: "And we're going to turn now to a woman who sought the source of strength and survival . . . and found it. Early this year, Anne Heck got a phone call that would change her life forever. She learned that she was going to go to court to face the man whose brutal acts might have shattered her life fourteen years ago."

A video clip gave viewers the backstory of the rape and a little history of my life from the incident to the present, as well as details about how the DNA match had occurred. I felt my heart beating in my chest and focused on my breathing, bringing it to a slow, steady rhythm as I awaited the first question. I reminded myself to speak slowly, to pause and be purposeful so my responses would be clear and succinct.

Sawyer began her interview asking how I'd felt in the courtroom, facing the man who raped me. I told her about the day I declared my year of strength and how that led to the call from Detective Newsome saying the rapist had been identified. The interview lasted only about five minutes, but it offered ample time to share what I felt would leave viewers with feelings of empowerment and hope: emphasizing that we're always at choice, encouraging them to state their intentions out loud, and highlighting the power of focus.

As stagehands readied the space for their next guest, Matt Damon, Tom and the children came out from the greenroom where they were greeted by Sawyer and had their photos taken. I felt satisfied I had agreed to appear on national television. It was an opportunity to publicly claim my strength and resilience. In my determination to stand in my power, the interview was one more action toward that end.

Numerous people contacted me in the aftermath of being in the public eye—aunts, uncles, and cousins who had never known my story and strangers who were touched by it. Amidst all the uplifting responses, I toyed with the idea of writing a book about my experience, about my prayer for strength and the amazing way all had subsequently unfolded. But I felt exhausted on many levels and chose to step out of the spotlight to give myself a much-needed rest. It had been a year of taking risks, of stretching myself and holding faith in a strength I had only imagined. Writing a book remained only a thought.

To my dismay, the strength that got me through the court appearance and media interviews began to crumble in the wake of it all. In the winter following my court appearance, I got bronchitis and spent weeks getting over it. My physical and emotional resilience diminished, and I began to feel I'd lost any ground I'd gained. An array of emotions had emerged as I navigated my "year of strength," but I'd allowed very few of them to express. It was just a matter of time before things erupted.

Anger was the first emotion to surface, and its sticky tendrils latched onto situations or people that strained my tenuous sense of well-being.

One such situation arose from my court appearance. The day before the hearing, as our family drove north, we had stopped at my parents' home for a visit. Mom and Dad were not ones to initiate conversations about the rape; it was a topic they'd rather avoid. That day, however, I invited them to the sentencing.

"You're welcome to come join me in the courtroom," I said. "I'd be happy to have you there." I explained that for me this was an opportunity for healing.

There wasn't an immediate response.

Mom and Dad sat in their respective chairs on opposite ends of the living room. I sat on the couch, Tom by my side.

"Do you feel you've ever gotten over this?" I asked, looking at Mom. She began to tear up and didn't say anything.

"What do you think, Janey?" Dad prodded. "Let's drive up."

"Oh, I don't know, Paul."

And that was that. Nothing more said. It was understood they wouldn't attend.

After the hearing, as my emotions surfaced, my parents became my scapegoats. Suddenly, I decided they had abandoned me when I went to court. I sensed they wanted to sweep my rape neatly under a carpet. I couldn't fault them for this; I had wished numerous times that I could neaten up my life with a broom and a large heavy rug. I recalled my dad's words of some fourteen years ago, the Christmas after the rape. "Pull up your bootstraps; put on a happy face," he told me. At the time, I'd resented what felt an insensitive response to my emotional turmoil. I felt the same resentment about my parents' absence at the hearing. Questions spun in my head: *Why couldn't they be there to support me? Just try to listen or understand? Ask how I'm doing? Don't they see how stressful all this is for me?* One tendril of anger had attached to my parents and was being well fed as I stirred anger into my story.

Years later, conversations with Mom would reveal that though I'd invited them to the court proceedings, I hadn't clearly stated my *desire* for them to be there. She and Dad had felt I was protecting them and didn't really want them to come, that perhaps I would feel responsible for them during my statement to the court. And she was right; at that time, it seemed too much to ask of them, so I was vague about my invitation. I'm certain I had doubts about having them in the courtroom. I had felt relieved that I wasn't responsible for that added layer of consideration on court day.

However, in the weeks after my court appearance, the more I focused on my outrage, the less able I was to lay it down. I found myself fuming at Dad for being so unfeeling, angry at Mom for not being emotionally present when I most needed her. My bitterness seethed out in everyday situations with my children or friends. I could barely keep it contained.

My anger seemed unreasonable. It had, after all, been fifteen years since the rape. I recalled the therapy group I'd attended years earlier and the woman who'd suffered for fifteen years from her experience of sexual violence. I'd felt frightened hearing that and imagining a future of anger and angst. I'd refused to believe that could be my experience. But the mining of my past to write the victim statement, then sharing my story with the media and facing the perpetrator had created a tidal wave of emotions that could no longer be kept at bay. Though I felt my intense upset might flood out my positive intentions, I continued practicing affirmative prayer and paying close attention to the messengers that came my way.

18

Magic

Will Rockingbear taught me to pay attention. After my soul retrieval in 2004, I joined one of Will's circles, and for six years I traveled weekly on Wednesdays—two hours round trip—to sit around the fire with eight other community members and this generous and wise Cherokee medicine man.

Will had sparkling eyes—bright blue—that radiated powerfully above sunken cheekbones. He wore Native-style button-up shirts in cheerful colors with fine satin ribbons sewn across the seams. His medicine bag, a well-loved fabric satchel of faded browns and blues, was always discreetly placed close by his side at the fire. Earth Green Medicine Lodge was where I learned to listen to messengers and came to know—or perhaps remember—the magic of fire.

Will reminded me of Gramp, Mom's father. Like Gramp, he spoke slowly, carefully, his words strong and gentle. I remembered one Christmas visit with my grandfather, our family all tucked around the fireplace in his back room. When Gramp's fire was strong and hot, he took a small round canister from the mantle, twisted off the top, and sprinkled a handful of Rainbow

Flame Crystals across the embers. They burnt bright red, purple, and blue and were beautiful. It's there I began to perceive fire as magic.

Upon entering Earth Green Medicine Lodge, we would smudge ourselves with sage. Smudging is a purifying ceremony that symbolizes the act of letting go of what isn't needed. Community members would then seat themselves on cushions surrounding a large bear pelt in the center of the medicine room. The fire—a candle—was always lit in the center of the altar.

Will was not a man of many words, but those he shared were clear, potent, and memorable. He spoke of conversations he'd had with deceased elders and spirit guides as if they existed in our current physical reality; for him there was no separation. He listened deeply in our conversations, had an uncanny ability to pinpoint core issues needing attention, and addressed such issues with a question or statement that greatly simplified whatever was seemingly difficult or painful.

Members of our Wednesday night circle were responsible for setting the altar, serving water, drumming, offering teachings and healings, and leading the pipe ceremony—an opportunity to share the smoking of a sacred pipe while expressing prayers and gratitude. Through these tasks we were taught to love and be gentle with ourselves and others, to feel gratitude, and to live our sacred lives by paying attention and taking proper action.

There were no Rainbow Flame Crystals at Earth Green Medicine Lodge, no red and purple flames. But around our ceremonial fire I repeatedly witnessed equally beautiful and profound transformation.

One particular Wednesday, I'd spent the afternoon in turmoil. Knowing that I couldn't hide my anger and upset in the circle, I nearly bagged the idea of driving up the mountain. But I'd joined the circle to seek healing, and if I wasn't willing to show up when I felt vulnerable, I might as well drop out and abandon my pursuit. So I carpooled to the lodge. With red swollen eyes, I sat in silence most of the trip. Others asked if they might help. I couldn't find words to explain. I would wait for safe and sacred space, a place that held the magic of fire.

In the few weeks before that day's circle, I'd been feeling anxious and irritable. Working through the anger I felt—toward my family and myself—had been exhausting. I was hesitant to take this to the medicine lodge. I didn't like the thought of losing control in circle. I still viewed emotional upset as weakness, and the intensity of my upset that day was astounding. The emotional tendrils that had latched onto my mom and dad had shaken me up. If anything could transform my angst, it would be ceremonial fire. That night I decided to ask for help.

I placed my cushion on the south edge of the circle, Chad on my left, Elana to my right, Jennie's sweet smile directly across from me, and good eye contact with Rockingbear. I sat comfortably upon my cushion and smoothed a blanket across my lap, making sure to weave my blanket corners with those of my neighbors—a circle complete. We began, as always, by calling in the four directions—a prayerful honoring of all our relations, an invitation for them to come sit with us, and an opportunity to express gratitude to Creator, to our ancestors, and to our guides in the spirit world.

In the center of our circle atop the bear rug lay an altar cloth of colorful Mexican fabric. On this were carefully placed altar items that would more than likely reveal a message for one or several of us during the circle. The altar keeper arrived early on circle night, energetically cleared the space, lit the fire, and listened closely to what medicine pieces called to be placed on the altar. Four tiny pottery bowls adorned the corners of the altar cloth, each filled with sacred medicine: cedar, salt, water, and corn. A softball-sized snowflake obsidian sphere sat in the west exuding a sense of calm and groundedness. To its side, someone had placed a jade necklace and a small heart-shaped stone. In the north was a single bear claw alongside a bundle of red fabric tied with thin leather twine. A large quartz crystal sat in the east, and in the south was a sizable reflective sheet of mica topped with the tiny skull of a mouse.

I felt anxious and impatient sitting on my cushion. Some fearful beast was knocking around inside of me, and I was desperate to extricate myself from it. While I was typically clear in articulating what was happening for me, my feelings at that moment were so foreign and magnified that I couldn't find words to explain them. I sat and sobbed with a fear and upset that felt bigger than me and wanted only to find its way out.

Staring into the fire prompted me to pay attention to what was before me. There, in the south, directly in front of my seat, was the mouse skull. *There are no accidents*, I thought. Its eye sockets were hollow, its cheekbones extremely delicate. I was reminded again of Gramp's home where, perched atop his kitchen doorframe, was a tiny wooden mouse, its leather tail drooping down toward my curious childhood eyes. Gramp would reach up, pluck the mouse's plump belly, and place him in my outreached hands. There I adored the mouse until it was returned to its pinnacle above the sink and dishes. I silently asked the fire what medicine the mouse held.

The answer came surprisingly fast, as if someone was sitting on my shoulder whispering in my ear. "Mouse energy is about scrutiny, discovering new meanings, new perspectives," the fire responded. I sat for a moment, unclear what this meant and how or if it might address what was screaming for attention.

Rockingbear sat in silence, his head slightly bowed, slowly rubbing his bare scalp with his right hand. He didn't seem to notice I was in turmoil.

Suddenly he looked my way and spoke. "You don't need to know the *how*," he said. "Where does the energy need to move?"

His unexpected inquiry gave me something to focus on. I closed my eyes and retreated into myself, feeling the discontented energy within me and asking where it wanted to go. I knew immediately how to answer. "The energy wants to move up and out the top of my head," I said.

Rockingbear came over and knelt beside me. Another community member brought smudge and an eagle feather. Eagle feathers are sacred; they're often used to brush away negative spirits or disease from the spiritual body to support healing of the physical body. The feather was incredibly strong; its forceful sweeping up my spine was accompanied by an inner sense of energy pulling together and rocketing through the top of my head. I felt perceptions shift and new awareness settle in. The released energy was guided to the fire to be transformed. Gradually my angst and tears subsided, and I had a clear vision of a small frightened girl curled up inside me.

"Who's there?" Rockingbear asked.

"It's me," I replied. I felt sadness and compassion for this young part of me that was fearful and desperate for healing. I was also suddenly aware that my anger and upset weren't really about my family; they were about not giving myself the loving attention I craved. My parents hadn't abandoned me. I had abandoned me. I hadn't honored my emotions, hadn't recognized the gentle, consistent support I needed from within. Instead, I had plowed forward just to get beyond the pain. I had never taken time to see and emulate the caring perspective of a loved one, of a parent, of a friend . . . to give this love to my hurting, needful self.

I'd received similar messages before, yet obviously I needed another reminder. The shift in perception seemed to resolve my imbalance. I sensed the little girl uncurling herself, feeling less fear and more hope. In that moment, balance seemed within reach and healing entirely possible. I had some work to do: it was time to pay attention to my needs and to respond with compassionate action.

I turned my gaze to the tiny mouse skull sitting atop the mica and to the flames of the fire that now seemed to burn with more brilliance than before. The fire had, once again, produced magic, and Mouse had gifted me with new perspective.

"Many thanks to Mouse," I prayed aloud. "And deepest gratitude to my grandfathers." I smiled deeply, fully.

19

Fear

I was grateful for the insight that a young part of me needed gentle compassion, but caring for myself in this way required more attention than I was willing to give. Mothering demanded most of my time and energy, and I easily fell into a pattern of pushing myself to do more than was physically possible, approaching life like a marathon. Inevitably this approach resulted in more anger and upset—painful reminders to be more gentle with myself. On those days, I'd load up my bike, head to the parkway, and let the tension roll off my shoulders as I pedaled familiar roads and breathed in fresh air. Cycling remained my go-to for restoring energy and boosting my spirit. Yet I didn't do enough of it, or of other things that might have helped. I tended not to heed my body's messages until its whispers became cries.

It was the fall of 2007 when once again I felt a river of emotion begin to overflow its banks. I'd been sandbagging my feelings, even as I'd addressed my anger as best I could. But that autumn I felt deluged with rage, grief, and confusion. My sleep was disrupted, my days long and draining. I needed to dive in and rectify things at a much deeper level.

I still sat every week with Will and the circle community at the medicine lodge. As well, I'd begun to see a therapist again. My issue wasn't specific. In a sea of emotions, I was searching for an island where I could stand on solid ground, collect myself, and gather confidence to walk through the mire. Perhaps some inner work pinpointing the source of my distress and using EMDR to resolve it would be helpful—and it was. But I was seeking more. It felt imposing to bring this work to the medicine lodge. Though I trusted that circle, I wanted a small nurturing container with only women. So I contacted Sharon.

Sharon was Rockingbear's spirit sister; they shared a soul connection, and she had been mentored by him for years. Sharon facilitated women's personal growth circles from her home in Asheville. I'd met her several years back at a workshop where she presented teachings about death and dying. Drawn to her warm, nurturing spirit, I'd kept her phone number on a slip of paper in my purse, knowing I'd be calling her when the time was right.

Three other women had joined me for Sharon's twelve-week circle. Our first morning together, I felt exhausted, raw, with tears at the ready. Anxious about showing up in such a sensitive state, I hadn't slept well the night before.

Sharon's altar was set with a tall wooden goddess statue with hands reaching toward the heavens, a heart-shaped rose quartz crystal nestled in colorful wool roving, and fresh flowers in an opaque blue glass vase. Sun poured into the tiny studio and brightened the pale yellow walls. Sheer curtains filtered the light and moved ever so gently with the morning's breath. The room smelled faintly of sage and sweetgrass. Sharon was in her early fifties, with long auburn hair, rosy cheeks, and a warm smile.

She opened the circle with a series of prayers. When it was my turn to share during introductions, I was weepy and stumbled over my words. Sharon responded, her words hushed but explicit. "It'd be good to invite your fear to the kitchen table," she said. She looked me in the eyes. "It's not as scary as you think. You can do this."

"I'm tired, Sharon," I whined. I hated whining, but at that moment my body hurt, my emotions were on tilt, and I didn't want to work on my issues. I felt frustrated, disappointed, and angry that I'd invested nearly twenty years in healing and still wasn't done with the pain and angst. All due to being sidetracked by sexual violence. I knew this wasn't a good direction to focus my energy, but the fatigue of the emotional work felt like a heavy weight on my shoulders—and on my hips. Yes, the burden fell most certainly on my hips.

Sharon encouraged me to embrace my emotions and find ways to connect more deeply with them. I trusted her judgment, and by the time I left the circle that day I felt inspired to dive into the work. I just needed to find a path that felt right for me.

I had tried journaling. For years, I'd channeled confusion or upset onto paper until all was encased neatly in perfect word packages. But word packets no longer worked; they were too small and inadequate for the immensity of my emotions.

I had also spent time with clay, trying to mold my emotions into a vessel or sculpture that could inform me, but the outcome felt empty, void of insight or meaning. So I set my intention on finding an artistic outlet that offered healing while also bringing joy. As with my first visit to a therapist years ago, I was looking to laugh my way to wholeness.

So it was that I found myself playing with dolls.

Fear

As a child, I rarely played with dolls. Mom had given me a floppy overstuffed cloth doll with a plastic head, hands, and feet when I was a toddler. She sewed multiple outfits for the doll—a bright pink woolen jacket, floral dresses, sun hats, and underwear. Sometimes I dressed the doll to display on my bed or dresser, but I wasn't much interested in playing house with her. I preferred being outdoors, riding my bicycle, being active. When indoor play was called for, I focused on creative pursuits—sewing, drawing, and playing piano.

Though playing with dolls was not my passion, I loved tiny things. When I was seven years old, my parents made me a dollhouse. Dad designed and cut it out of plywood, hinged two large front doors, made windows, staircases, and closets, and painted it white with a green roof. It stood nearly as tall as me—a beautiful three-story home. The front of the house had green shutters and tiny window boxes from which sprouted inch-high pastel-colored plastic flowers. The doors opened outward to reveal three floors covered with upholstery fabric or velvet for carpet and gold-flecked drawer lining paper for linoleum floors in the kitchen and bath. Mom had wallpapered each room with lovely quilting fabric, and tiny framed pictures hung on the walls.

I spent many childhood hours collecting miniature things and adoring the reproductions that could be made at this minuscule scale. And I crafted my own small creations for the dollhouse—teeny wrapped packages, yellow pencils fashioned out of toothpicks, mini wire hangers for the closets.

Aside from the dollhouse, I created other miniature things— tiny paper cuttings, small felted items, Advent calendars, and fabric collages. And I collected small objects to display on the shelves in my bedroom: little glass animals and a myriad of nature items like acorns, seashells, sticks, and stones. Outdoors

I created fairy villages with soft bright green mosses, stick structures, and grass thatching.

So, in my mid-forties, I revisited the world of tiny and began obsessing over art dolls. I sat for hours searching the Internet for these tiny renditions of human form, fascinated at how simple structures and materials held such powerful expression of emotions: the suggestion of surprise in a face, joy or exuberance in a body's limbs, or sadness in the tilt of a head.

For weeks I studied doll artists and photos of their work. Though I wanted to make a doll, I didn't know how to begin and wouldn't allow myself to indulge in a practice that wasn't going to produce something as wondrous as the pictures I'd seen, so I continued to look. Tom, who is way more comfortable experimenting with new endeavors, was troubled watching my process.

"What exactly intrigues you about the dolls?" he asked. "Are you planning to make one?" His questions soon transitioned to "When are you going to make one?" and "What will yours be made from?" After several weeks of questioning, Tom decided that the only way I'd make a doll was if he gave me an assignment. "I think it's time to make your own doll. I challenge you to stop looking at photos and to make your own. I'll give you twenty-four hours," he said. Then he left the house with clear expectation that I would unveil my creation upon his return.

And I did.

I drew my first doll body on a piece of white printing paper. Two templates were cut from some unbleached muslin I found buried in my blanket chest. I sewed the edges, turned the fabric inside out, and stuffed her. I then dressed her in wild-patterned pants and a gold tunic tied at the waist with a piece of yarn. I hand-painted her face and sewed colorful yarn atop her head. She had no support in her neck, so she was a droopy-headed doll, but she was complete. I named her Cindy, as she reminded me of my spunky friend from graduate school whose name I adopted the day I was raped.

Cindy wasn't like any doll I'd seen on the Internet. She was my original design, and I felt satisfaction that I'd been midwife to her creation. I felt an emotional connection with her, perhaps because I'd made her myself, or because of her bright clothing and large knowing eyes, or because I enjoyed the reminder of Cindy. Whatever the reason, looking at her empowered me. She was colorful and strong (except for her neck), and she had character. Yes, I loved her.

Around the same time, I came upon the website of doll artist Barb Kobe, who facilitated a virtual circle of women making dolls to assist their personal healing journeys. The description of her class mentioned the medicine wheel, a sacred symbol of indigenous people that is used for, among other things, the process of transformation. My familiarity with the medicine wheel from sitting in the Earth Green circle, my attraction to dolls, and the path of healing felt like a perfect combination. I called Barb and joined her circle.

Nearly twenty women from all parts of the globe connected through an online group, sharing personal stories and photos of their dolls. Barb provided a map for participants to navigate their healing journey. Inspired by her suggestion that the map could be likened to the medicine wheel, I promptly adopted this symbol to direct my own process. Years later, I offered my own workshops using doll making for transformation and created a medicine wheel diagram to guide participants (see image on the next page).

My healing doll journey began on the east side of the medicine wheel and moved clockwise around the circle (though this is not the starting point, nor is clockwise the direction for all people). East equates with new beginnings, with springtime and clear vision. The doll of the east embodies the divine mother—a guardian who will watch over and guide the coming journey, a symbol of protection, hope, and encouragement. I "called in" this doll of the east by sitting quietly and asking for her essence or spirit to make itself known. Barb suggested asking the doll what colors, textures, and expressions (body and facial) would best convey her spirit. I took notes, drew sketches, and from there had a good sense of an image. Combining polymer clay, paint, and fiber, I brought her into form. Her name was *Gentle One*.

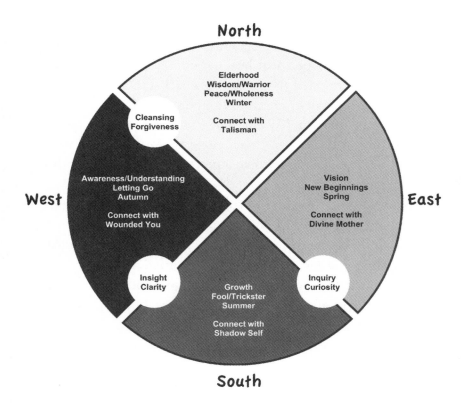

Doll Healing Medicine Wheel

© Anne Heck 2020

Fear

Gentle One hung on the wall next to my sewing table, the soft green fabric of her robe tucked around her peaceful face, her golden hands open to offer whatever assistance was needed. This guardian's tiny figure—a mere fifteen inches tall—exuded a sense of calm and gave me confidence that I would be supported as I explored my emotions more deeply. It wasn't long before I felt ready to meet my shadow as I moved into the south end of the medicine wheel.

The south direction is associated with the summer season, with growth, and with the fool or trickster as our teacher. On the doll journey, the south is where we connect with our shadow self. This concept of shadow is most often attributed to psychologist Carl Jung. It's the part of our personality that's relegated to our unconscious, where it exerts control over us in ways we're not aware of. The shadow consists of parts we've pushed aside rather than looked at.

As I visioned, sketched, and journaled to connect with the doll of the south, I became more aware of the part of me that felt unsettled, reactive, and pained. These symptoms were outer manifestations of an inner imbalance, and I felt ready to know my inner terrain well enough to work with it rather than against it.

I devoted months to creating a shadow doll. It was during the making of this doll that I joined Sharon's circle and was encouraged, at our first gathering, to explore my fear. But fear did not surface in my doll work at the time. My first shadow doll was a wire mesh shell on which I glued words to express my feelings: unworthy, empty, unfulfilled. The doll's head was a clay mask representing only half a face. This half had a smiling expression. The other half of her face was missing. She didn't seem to have a name for herself, so I called her *Mesh Mess* for the messy process of working with wire. I sensed this doll represented only my surface experience, because as I worked on her,

155

emotions bubbled up to let me know something was brewing at a deeper level. Though I couldn't access the core emotion, I was patient and felt certain it would surface.

Barb encouraged participants to dialogue with their dolls, to see what messages or lessons they had to share. This, she suggested, was best done through dominant/non-dominant handwriting. Using my dominant hand, I wrote questions in my journal, switching the pen to my non-dominant hand to answer them. Each hand enables access to different functions of the brain. The analytical function formulates the questions; the creative, artistic, intuitive function offers responses. Holding a pen in my left hand felt awkward and cumbersome. But I got the hang of it and was surprised that writing this way accessed a wise, informative part of me.

As I created *Mesh Mess*, I had vacillated between resistance and tears. The wire was difficult to shape and would split in places, poking painfully into my fingers. Once the doll was complete, I resented her presence; she felt rigid and detached. As I dialogued with her, she revealed a theme of empty versus full. It took a bit of journaling to understand that this theme was simply a different perspective on what I'd been addressing for years: my sense of loss after being raped and my continued search for wholeness. Empty and Full played leading roles in the theater of my mind.

After finishing the shadow doll, my head ached and I felt heavy all day. The next morning, I woke up at four o'clock and pulled out my journal to dialogue with the doll, and this poem emerged.

Playmates

Emptiness and Fullness came together for a day.
Bleak, silent void of Empty did not know what to say.

Overflowing with abundance, Full grabbed Empty by the
hand
And led her off to play in her imaginary land.

Drained of joyful emotion, Empty sat down in her path.
This, of course, seemed funny, and Full began to laugh.
Tears welled up in Empty's eyes; her chest began to heave.
So Full sat down beside her, allowing her to grieve.

Full held Empty in her arms, watched the tears that had
    no end.
Then she realized the irony she saw within her friend.
Why, Empty wasn't empty, she was really FULL of tears,
And just needed to express the pain she'd held for all
    these years.

And she needed Full's compassion at this time when all
    seemed bleak.
So Full held Empty close and wiped her teary cheek.
At this moment, Empty melted in the kindness she received
And found that she could feel not so heavily aggrieved.

The healing moment gifted Empty with a valuable life tool
And it helped her to know that she, too, could feel full.
The sad, unworthy feelings Empty now could rise above
Because she was connected with what she knew was love.

As it turned out, *Mesh Mess* was the first of three iterations of
my shadow doll. I'd expected to move promptly to the north end
of the medicine wheel, where I would create my talisman, a doll
that symbolized resolution with my shadow self and a feeling
of inner peace. Instead, I was humbled by the depth of emotion
exposed in the shadow doll process and realized I would have
to practice patience—for the umpteenth time. It seemed the

dolls were saying, "You asked for our help, which means we're in charge of the process. So you'll have to let go and allow us to lead."

Within a month, I'd begun work on a second shadow doll. *Mesh Mess* hadn't brought me a sense of completion, and I knew I could take the work deeper. I began making a reproduction of my traumatized body from the day I was raped. I thought this might identify the core emotion the shadow doll represented and that I needed to release. I made the doll from muslin dyed a light skin color. I sewed a miniature version of my favorite blue biking shirt and eight-panel biking shorts to fit the doll's body. Her right arm was bent behind her back—as mine had been—and I intended to embellish her with cuts, bruises, and injuries. But I couldn't. The image in my mind was nightmarish, and creating it with my own hands was bringing me too close to the horrible reality it had been. I abandoned the doll. I knew I'd need to face my emotions at some point, but this wasn't gentle. It would have to wait.

A couple weeks later, the shadow began to take a new form. This new doll was made of lavender-and-white batiked fabric splattered with orange-red stains positioned in places I had sustained the greatest injury. Her legs ran in a puddle from her torso, unable to provide support for standing or walking. Her hands were upright close to her chest, protecting her body. Her face was mangled with eyes protruding, expressing horror. As I created this third shadow doll, my sleep was disrupted, I was prone to headaches, and I felt queasy. In so many ways she mirrored my emotions on the day I was raped. Her name, she told me, was *Fear.*

Once *Fear* was complete, I placed her on my desk and sat with her daily, attempting to connect through dominant/non-dominant journaling. *Fear* was ugly, uncomfortable to look at. I was disgusted by her, but I kept her in full view and tried multiple times to dialogue with her, without success. I sensed that my disgust created resistance and blocked communication. One morning as I approached my desk, the doll seemed to scream for my attention. This was the first time I'd felt a strong pull in her direction, so I immediately grabbed my journal and wrote with my right hand, "Do you have something you'd like to share?"

I took a breath and settled into a receptive mind-set with the pen in my left hand. Without hesitation, the doll replied, "You are not your fear."

"Okay," I wrote, somewhat curtly. "Anything else?"

"You think you're your fear, but fear is only a small part of who you are," she replied. "Keep in mind that you have far more capacity, skill, and wisdom than you're aware of. Because of this, you're capable of overcoming whatever makes you *feel* afraid."

I'd never considered fear as a small part of the whole. When it had my attention, it felt all-consuming and inescapable. The hip pain, breathlessness, and anxious thoughts together composed the entirety of what I knew as fear. However, I had practiced affirmations and engaged in empowering activities like cycling that had resulted in more confidence and ease; perhaps these were the skills *Fear* spoke of. *I am not my fear*, I repeated to myself. It was a powerful reminder.

Had I engaged in this process even five years earlier, I'd have dismissed the doll's messages as whimsy and mental fabrication. But being dismissive and skeptical hadn't helped me access greater emotional wisdom. My experience communicating with dolls was very real—so real and spiritually informative, in fact, that I would continue making dolls for the next seven years. Over that time, I created a dozen dolls: one for each direction and others that came in to teach me a specific lesson. (You can see all the dolls on my website at www.anneheck.com.)

A Fierce Belief in Miracles

As days passed and I considered *Fear*'s message, I was inspired to acknowledge my strengths. I imagined myself filled with stability, wisdom, and courage. I brought *Fear* (the doll) and my own fear to the kitchen table as Sharon had suggested, and began to pay attention to what initiated my fear and what strengths I could draw on to overcome it. I gave positive messages to myself and got on my bike more often. My sense of disgust for the doll lessened; my respect for her grew. I sensed her resilience as my resilience. At times when I felt fearful, I would see the doll's face in my mind's eye and hear her reminder: *You are not your fear.*

20

Vulnerability

One morning I placed my newly completed doll *Fear* on the altar in Sharon's circle. I explained that I was doing my best to understand the fearful part of me. I felt angry that ugliness was surfacing in my doll making and that my physical body was still stubbornly holding onto its pain. I don't recall the exact words I shared in that session, but I well remember Sharon's response.

"I invite you to practice some self-compassion," she said.

I turned defensive. *What does compassion have to do with my angst and upset? How could it possibly ease my pain and anxiety?* I kept these thoughts to myself, and though I don't remember my reply, I'm certain my frustration was apparent.

Sharon was patient, as always. "Self-compassion," she explained, "is a way of relating to yourself kindly."

She went to her corner cupboard where she kept an assortment of medicine pieces. From the dark wooden shelves she retrieved a beautiful white porcelain statue of the goddess Kwan Yin, draped in long robes, with a most peaceful expression. The goddess was adorned with an elegant headdress and a delicate line of pearls at her neck and cradled a willow branch in her arms.

"I invite you to sit with Kwan Yin for a bit," Sharon said. "She's known as the mother of compassion, and I feel she has some things to teach you. Take the doll home with you, and ask her to teach you about compassion."

I was both resistant and curious. At home I placed the statue on the corner of my desk, where I could see her daily. On researching Kwan Yin, I learned that she vowed to free all beings from suffering, and that her willow branch was used to heal people's illnesses or bring fulfillment to their requests. What she could offer me wasn't clear. Numerous mornings, I whispered my prayer to her, "Please show me what I need to know about compassion."

A few weeks later, my anger became magnified. I hadn't gained any insight into compassion, and I'd started to resent Kwan Yin's presence. Relating kindly to myself seemed self-indulgent. I didn't want to disappoint Sharon, but I was ready for the statue to be out of my house. And I wasn't keen on attending the next circle meeting, either. My irritation felt as if it was forcing itself out of my pores. I had no interest in hearing about compassion or forgiveness or whatever other gentle path Sharon was likely to suggest.

Once our group was seated in the studio, Sharon glanced at me, then nodded. I knew she sensed my upset. She opened the circle by lighting the candle at the center of our altar and calling in the directions. She then turned to me.

"What do you bring to our circle today, Anne?"

I looked her straight in the eye and replied firmly, "I don't want to hear anything about forgiveness or compassion. I'm angry." Then I burst into tears.

It was a brash way to show up in such a gentle space, but I was at the end of my emotional rope. I needed to rant, and I wanted to be heard. Sharon assured me she was listening. Again, conversation turned to compassion, but I didn't want to hear it.

Sharon took another path. She encouraged me to try an "anger bath" to transform my emotions, and gave me a recipe which called for apple cider vinegar, essential oils she would lend me, and a quartz crystal. Though it sounded like more New Age woo, I agreed to try it because I trusted Sharon. She invited me to state my request to the fire, our altar candle that still burned brightly. I spoke my prayer aloud into the tiny flame, asking to gently transform my anger into peace. My women comrades nodded in support as they held space for me to discover my perfect path to this end.

That evening I pulled vinegar from the cupboard and a quartz crystal from my altar, and assembled Sharon's essential oils in a line on the side of my tub. I ran my bath, gently placing the quartz on the bottom of the tub and counting the prescribed drops of oil. Once I sank into the inviting warmth, I surrendered to whichever angels or spirits might offer reprieve.

The following morning, before the family woke, I sat journaling my feelings into a spiral-bound notebook and was mysteriously drawn to part of my story that I'd previously overlooked. I say mysteriously because this name simply fell out on the page as I was writing: Sandi Goodwin.

Two years prior, I'd entered Sandi's name and address into the contacts on my computer after the hearing. In the notes section under her name, I wrote "the other woman." Sandi, in West Virginia, had encountered Terry McDonald the day before I did. Detective Newsome had told me the details of her story.

Sandi was sitting on her porch swing on a sunny afternoon when Terry approached her. He hit her in the face, then raped her. Her five-year-old daughter, witnessing the violence from behind the screen door, promptly ran to the kitchen, climbed up on the counter to the phone, dialed 911, then hid in the closet. Terry stole Sandi's red car that day and drove through the night to Manassas, Virginia, where he encountered me the next morning.

My journal provided a safe container as I explored "the other woman." *What a horrible experience,* I thought. *How did Sandi and her daughter manage to get through it? Had they been able to heal from the trauma?* I was particularly touched by the girl—the frightened little girl. And I cried—no, sobbed. I sobbed for Sandi, and even more for the innocent girl hurt in the process. Suddenly, I had become both of them: the injured woman and the frightened young girl. Though we'd never met, I felt bonded with these two females; we'd been battered by the same hands, threatened by the same voice. I felt their grief, their frustration, their rage. I wanted somehow to acknowledge their hurt, to offer them comfort and support. And I realized how much I needed this myself—the kindness, the gentleness—how much I longed to be comforted. The transformation I'd sought was at hand. Whether it had been the anger bath or, in her unassuming ways, Kwan Yin's presence, I felt I was at last traveling the path of self-compassion.

In the weeks that followed, I created a *Compassionate Mother* doll from feelings and images I associated with Kwan Yin and Sandi and her daughter. This doll of the west embodied motherly love, exuding kindness and a gentle spirit. I devoted hours to beading her layered skirt and finely knitting her scarf with toothpicks. I made her leather slippers from an old pair of gloves that had been my mother's. Her creation required tenderness and undivided attention—attention which soon extended beyond the making of a doll. I burned with desire to experience this type of nurturing for myself. I needed and deserved such compassionate care. I was humbled in gratitude for the lesson I was learning about self-compassion. I asked Tom to take more responsibility with the children. I began to nurture myself more often—with a warm bath, some evening reading, a yoga class, or tea with a friend. My anger dissipated, and I felt more energized and refreshed. This was the experience of self-compassion.

In Sharon's circle a few weeks later, I was ready to engage another issue that challenged me. The morning was damp and foggy, and a space heater was warming the small studio. I removed my shoes, cleared myself with smudge, and entered the circle. Five of us sat together on floor cushions, blankets across our laps, a candle lighting the altar. I felt emotionally stronger that day; nonetheless, this issue had haunted me for some time, and I felt sensitive about what the group might reflect back to me.

That I was challenged by this emerging piece is an understatement. My lack of resolution on this topic was like static interrupting a favorite radio station—background noise that slowly and continually pulled on my energy. I had expected it to become clear on its own, but as time passed, it was evident I needed help.

When it was my turn to share, I said to the women, "I really want to understand the reason why I was raped. Not in the sense of 'why me?'—but I feel I may have been seeking something at age twenty-six that aligned me with an experience of trauma. I really want to understand this." The woman across the circle from me grimaced.

I had wrestled with this question when I wrote my victim impact statement. The statement had been an opportunity to apply meaning to the rape, and writing it had helped me immensely. Still, there was something that remained hidden from me, something I needed to know and understand.

"Can you share a bit more, so I have clarity about what you're asking?" Sharon said.

"The day I was raped, I got a clear message not to go down that gravel road. I had listened to that message and physically turned around to avoid whatever it was warning me about. But something called me back to that gravel road, and that's where I went, despite my initial feeling. This has been a point of confusion. Which voice should I have listened to? Why were there two voices? And why were they giving me conflicting information? I'm not confident I can trust my intuition."

Sharon sat patiently on her cushion, a Pendleton blanket across her knees. Her eyeglasses stared down her nose; her eyes, peering over the top of the frames, met mine.

"What I hear you saying is that you're uncertain how to discern your inner guidance from other voices in your head," she said.

"Yes, that's part of it. Was there a higher voice I was listening to that day? Was that the voice of my mind? Or was it the voice of my heart? How can I know which voice to trust?" I felt myself getting worked up, my breath faltering as my words tumbled out with a fury.

"Let's slow this down," Sharon instructed. "Tell me the details of that morning—the best you can remember."

"It was a Thursday morning in July," I began. "I sat at breakfast thinking about my good friend Ted and how much I admired his deep faith. I'd decided I would ride a route that Ted and I had ridden a few weeks earlier, setting my destination for a little bakery where we'd eaten lunch together. Over breakfast, I studied my bike map to identify the roads I'd taken when I was with Ted. I couldn't quite remember which road we'd taken to ride toward the bakery, but was sure I'd recognize it when I got out there." I paused, choosing my words carefully as I recalled a younger me.

"At that time in my life, I was looking for something, and Ted seemed to have it. Ted had a strong sense of who he was, and

I wanted the same thing. I wanted to trust something beyond just me. I wanted to feel the comfort in—the trust of—that support."

The other women sat quietly, their attention on my words. I took a breath, remembering how deeply I admired Ted's faith.

"Faith," I said. "I was seeking faith that day. I rode with that intention in mind."

The woman beside me breathed an affirmative "hmmmm."

My breath caught in my chest; my eyes began to burn as they filled with tears. I wasn't sure what was making me so emotional.

Sharon had her eyes locked on mine. I felt intense loving support from the other women. Sharon waited, honoring my process.

Faith. That's what I was looking for. Had I found it? My mind scanned back through years of searching, through letting go of my tight hold on logic and reasoning, testing the world of the unseen, discovering my own way of relating to Spirit, having prayers answered. The transformation had happened slowly, but it was undeniable. I had learned to trust in a power outside myself. I consulted with it daily. I relied on its blessings, offered it gratitude. And I felt supported; I could lean into Spirit in a way I had once only dreamed of. *Yes, I'd found faith.*

As this knowing began to take hold, I understood I had answered my own question. I'd had a purpose that day as I left for my bike ride—a desire to feel Spirit's presence in my life, to "find faith." I wanted to know with certainty that some divine power had my back. I'd received an internal warning signal to avoid that gravel road; I'd honored it and turned my bike around. But moments later, I received another intuitive signal that made me decide to take the gravel road anyway—and unknowingly pursue this life-altering journey.

I began sharing my thoughts aloud. "There were two

intuitive signals that day," I started. "The voice saying 'Don't take the gravel road' was my inner voice of protection telling me there was danger that way. The voice telling me 'Do take the gravel road' was the voice of my higher self letting me know this was my path to faith. At the time, I didn't have the discernment to know which voice was which. Still, my choice was to take that gravel road. Some part of me knew what it was doing."

I paused, taking a breath, breathing in this new awareness. "I've always thought these voices were in conflict, and because of this, I couldn't trust my intuition. I wasn't sure which voice to listen to. Now I get it."

I took another deep breath, to further ensure this awareness was sinking in. I wanted to leave circle that day with clarity and with confidence in my own guidance.

"Both voices were working to inform me. They weren't in conflict. It was information I needed in that moment, and based on the information—what I felt, what I heard—I made my choice. I took that gravel road."

Sharon nodded, a knowing expression on her face. My chest swelled with gratitude, tears streaming down my cheeks. With this new understanding, I'd cracked open a crucible of emotions—doubt and fear I'd held for years as I sought some uncharted mooring where I could anchor my trust. With the static cleared, I felt relieved and lighter. I anticipated a more comfortable relationship with my intuition.

Synchronistically, when I returned home that day, Ted, whom I hadn't heard from for over a year, had left a message on my voicemail.

PART THREE

.

21

Healer

"Have you ever considered becoming an energy healer?" Shirley asked.

Sharon had referred me to Shirley, who was also an apprentice of Rockingbear, as well as a nurse and a Healing Touch Practitioner. I'd just received a healing session from her, and lying on the table, I felt as peaceful as a still mountain lake. Her question, however, landed like a boulder on the water, disturbing the stillness of my lake.

"No, I haven't," I replied. My stomach turned, and chills ran up my arms. I felt a strange sensation of warmth and fear. *Look at me*, my mind said. *Why would someone ask a wounded person to heal them? I haven't been able to heal myself.*

"You have a body awareness and perception that I don't often find," Shirley said. "Not only does your body respond easily to energy manipulation, but your awareness would enable you to pick up on the energy of others and help them with their healing."

I felt swayed by the certainty in her voice, but my doubts were equally strong.

"How could I give others what I don't have myself?"

"You don't have to be healed to help others," Shirley explained. "You just need to have desire to do the work and willingness to hold space for healing to happen. I didn't do any healing here today. I just balanced the flow of energy so your body could heal itself."

I felt a flutter of excitement. I'd never considered energy healing as a vocation for myself. I recalled how my childhood friends and I had transformed my uncle's small bedroom at the back of Grandma's house into an infirmary. Its single bed with crisp white sheets was the patient's healing space. The bottom drawer of a mahogany dresser opened stiffly to reveal a toy doctor kit with a plastic syringe, stethoscope, hot water bottle, and container of brightly colored sugar pills. Leaning against the wall were two wooden fraternity paddles that looked like boat oars, with Greek symbols of my uncle's fraternity printed on each side. They were the perfect height for crutches for an eight-year-old, and I pretended to be a patient learning to walk. Up and down Grandma's long hallway I bounded on wooden legs, fast and efficient. I was the patient showing signs of resilience and healing.

Though I liked playing the patient and perfecting my crutch-walking skills, I secretly wanted to be the doctor. I imagined possessing extraordinary skill and powers that helped patients overcome their illnesses and injuries.

As an adult, I'd researched subtle energy extensively in pursuit of my own healing. Though not trained in how to manipulate energy, I was well-versed in the concept. And that afternoon, someone I barely knew had suggested I become a healer. *I could at least look into it . . .*

Later that week, I did some Internet research and called a local Healing Touch instructor to ask about becoming a practitioner. The conversation inspired me, and I was tempted to register for a class. But as I considered doing so, my gut began to tighten and I felt resistant.

Granted, the word "healer" seemed a misnomer for me, with my pained body. But there was something deeper. Years ago I'd heard my dad refer to chiropractic as "quackery." *That would make Healing Touch, by comparison, an extreme form of quackery,* I thought. Science had no evidence for its validity. And in my world, people became doctors, lawyers, schoolteachers—not healers.

Days went by, and I vacillated. I researched the effectiveness of energy healing, looking for scholarly work and double-blind studies. All I found were anecdotal accounts of manipulating energy to produce seemingly miraculous transformation. *But wait a minute,* I thought, *I know the effectiveness of energy healing from my own experience. Who am I trying to convince?* A week later, admittedly with a bit of defiance, I signed up for a Level 1 training with Healing Touch International.

At our first class, I learned that most of my classmates were nurses. With no medical background or perceived ability to heal others, I felt unsure of myself. Not long into our practice sessions, however, that shifted. I would move my hand slowly over my partner's body as the instructor directed, paying attention to how it felt—the temperature, the texture, and other sensations. I could discern where the body's energy was warm, where it was stifled or prickly or smooth, how the energy moved easily or not at all. *I can do this!* I had in fact been doing this for a long time in my own body, just as Shirley had suggested.

Since the rape, I'd devoted countless hours to workshops, retreats, and healing sessions with multiple practitioners, as well as home practice, meditation, and exercises. Over fifteen years, I'd been trained in or participated in over seventy alternative healing modalities including qigong, Quantum-Touch, Rolfing, Emotional Freedom Technique, Buteyko Breathing, and co-counseling. The knowledge I'd acquired about movement, musculature, breathing, and relaxation had unknowingly given me a deep awareness of my body and the subtle energies that affected it.

After two years and five levels of Healing Touch training, I felt confident in my skills. Certification required a practicum in which I would serve a hundred clients over a year's time. I bought a massage table and excitedly began spreading the word that I was offering healing sessions out of my home. I soon had a regular flow of clients.

Jamie came to see me on a cold, clear January afternoon. A college freshman, she'd been raped at school just three months earlier. My acupuncturist had referred her.

Jamie and I had spoken briefly by phone; mostly, I had listened. Her story was familiar. In my work as a crisis advocate and a healing practitioner in training, I'd been privy to numerous similar stories. Jamie's primary concern was tension headaches, but she also spoke of hip pain, sleeping difficulty, and what she described as "an emotional edge." Before the session began, as we sat across from each other at a small table in my living room, I began to feel the imbalances in her energy.

"Have you ever received energy work?" I asked.

"No." She fidgeted with a large onyx ring on her index finger. Her shoulders were tense, her chest tight, and her breathing shallow. Though she seemed fragile in the moment, Jamie was a runner, and I sensed she had tough, resilient qualities.

"Let me tell you a little about how I work. My goal is to provide you with balance and ease. I do this by moving energy, using light touch, like this," I said, reaching out to gently touch her shoulder. "Or I'll move energy with no touch, just manipu-lating the field around your body." I demonstrated by brushing my hand near her arm without touching it. "This balancing will allow energy to flow more efficiently and help your body do its own healing."

"Okay," she said. Her voice was gentle. She didn't look at me but stared down at her hands.

"I work intuitively, so once I get a sense of how things are moving in your body and what needs attention, I'll focus on freeing up compromised energy so all will flow better."

"Will I need to give you feedback about what I feel?" she asked.

"You're welcome to share what you're feeling, but it's most beneficial for clients to get out of their heads during a session. I invite you to focus on your breathing and relax as much as possible."

"Okay."

"I'd like to hear what your intention is for our time together. It might be different from when we spoke on the phone, so take a deep breath and feel into this moment. When you're ready, tell me what stands out as needing the most attention today."

Jamie sat with her eyes closed, still fumbling with her hands.

"I'd like to feel more clear," she said, this time looking at me. "I feel so distracted and confused lately."

"And if you felt more clear, what would that give you?"

She sat for a moment.

"If I'm more clear, I'm able to make decisions and get things done, and I can relax a little. So I guess life would be easier. I'd feel more peaceful."

"So, we're looking for a sense of peace, to feel relaxed," I reflected back to her.

"That would be nice."

"Great. Let's get started."

I guided Jamie from the living room into my healing space. Two of my dolls were displayed in the space: *Gentle One* and *Fear*. I invited Jamie to lie face up on the massage table as I placed a bolster beneath her knees. Her energy felt prickly, unsettled, particularly around her pelvis and hips. I held her feet until I felt the static dissipate and then began working with gentle touch, slowly but deliberately up her legs, allowing her body to find its own balance and ease. As I lightly touched her hips, I felt *Fear* nudge me. In my head, I began to converse with the doll.

My medicine dolls are displayed throughout my home, so there are always one or two in my presence. I'm interacting with them energetically on a daily basis. Hearing a message from the dolls is akin to seeing a library book on the coffee table and suddenly being aware it's overdue, or standing at the sink and sensing it's time to change the water filter. Passing by a doll, its energy might feel calm, or it might feel agitated as it tries to gain my attention. If the latter occurs, I do my best to make time to listen. In a healing session, it's easy to listen, because I'm already listening to the messages conveyed through the client's body.

"Hang out there a bit," *Fear* urged. "Connect her heart energy to her hips."

I lightly touched my left hand to Jamie's heart and suspended my right hand above her pelvis, slowly circling. The energy felt stifled; I wanted to feel it flowing.

When a client's symptoms felt familiar to me, my own body would buzz in resonance with the client's imbalance. I felt my chest tighten briefly—a reminder to breathe. As air filled my lungs, I imagined Jamie receiving the relaxing effect of a deep breath. Slowly her body began to respond, her chest and hips relaxing more deeply into the table, her energy becoming more fluid and peaceful. Jamie fell into a deep sleep, her mouth agape, softly snoring.

As she slept, I continued to smooth her energy, ending our session by holding her feet and silently offering a healing blessing, then allowing her to rest a bit before waking her. I thanked *Fear* for her assistance, then softly touched Jamie's shoulder, inviting her to move slowly and gently when she was ready.

Jamie sat up and looked at me directly. "That was amazing," she said. "I feel incredibly peaceful. I felt light-headed when you began to work on me, then I lost track of things. And now, I just feel relaxed."

"It sounds like your body did what it needed to support your intention. Good work focusing on your breath and allowing," I said.

I asked about her support system at school and encouraged her to find activities and a focus that could help her maintain the ease she currently felt. She thanked me for our session, and we parted ways.

22

Commitment

In late 2009, I completed my year of practicum training and became a full-time Healing Touch Practitioner, continuing to serve clients out of my home. I loved the work; it required me to be present, listen deeply, and practice being open and receptive. And sessions always led to people feeling more balanced and at ease. I debriefed with clients after each session, sharing information I'd perceived while working with them or messages that came through the dolls. As time passed, several women asked if I might offer group work or reflective circles where participants could learn and practice listening to themselves. It was not work I had anticipated, but with enough inquiries, I chose to begin facilitating two weekly circles, one open to the public, the other a closed group for those who wanted to venture more deeply. I was surprised by how much I enjoyed this work.

The struggle with my own health continued. The only physical activity I could still commit to faithfully was cycling. It not only exercised my body but also helped clear my mind and lift my spirit. In March of 2009, a few months before I'd finished my practicum, as I was taking a spin on the parkway, I had felt an inner call to participate in a vision quest.

In indigenous culture, a vision quest is a rite of passage consisting of a series of ceremonies facilitated by elders and supported by the community. The individual who's "questing" is led to a remote spot in nature such as a desert, forest, or hilltop to pray to Spirit for a vision that will identify their life's purpose, answer a burning question, or let them see how best to use their gifts. The quester typically sits in seclusion without food or water for four days and nights or until they receive their vision.

I had supported quests led by Rockingbear by helping cook meals for the community that gathered in ceremony. Sharon and Shirley were part of that community and had been mentored by Rockingbear to facilitate their own quests. The two of them began co-leading a women's vision quest circle in the fall of 2008, which I promptly joined. I felt a kinship with this circle of women who sought to connect more deeply with Spirit, and I wanted to make the most of the experience.

When someone feels called to quest, they approach the quest facilitator with their desire and with an offering of tobacco. The facilitator then prays with a pipe each day for four days as they smoke the gifted tobacco and consider the request, sitting in each of the four directions and listening to Spirit's response. If it's the will of Spirit, the facilitator offers their blessings to the seeker and agrees to watch over and protect them during the quest.

Committing to quest was not something I took lightly. I didn't look forward to a difficult undertaking that would be hard on my body, but something called loudly for me to take part in the ceremony. I expected that time spent in prayer on the quest would offer me clarity about my own healing and life purpose, two pieces that now seemed intertwined.

A Fierce Belief in Miracles

In mid-March, I visited Shirley at her home. We sat in her living room, chatting about my Healing Touch practice, which she had inspired. It was my first time in her home. The noonday sun brightened distant kitchen windows that looked out on a forest of newly budding trees—a promise of new growth. My gaze fell on several Native drums hung on the wall above long, low bookcases. I felt an inner stirring and longed to hear a rhythm that would resonate with my whole being, a rhythm that was uniquely mine and would inspire greater clarity and purpose.

Conversation soon turned to the quest. I placed in Shirley's hands a gift of tobacco wrapped in red wool fabric—a gesture that symbolized my request for support. Shirley pulled the bundle close to her heart, then leaned down and gently touched the floor as an expression of gratitude.

My request was simple. "Would you be willing to place me on the mountain and support my quest?"

Shirley again touched the red bundle to her heart. "Thank you for asking," she said, "and for being willing to do this work, for yourself and for all of us. I'll be sitting with it."

Though my physical activity had recently diminished due to pain and fatigue, and my body felt tired much of the time, I was ready to commit to whatever Spirit required of me to live with health and vitality, along with meaning and purpose. I hoped quest would deliver me to that imagined place.

Quest, as all true commitments, begins the moment you take action; handing tobacco to Shirley was the action that symbolized my commitment. I recalled Rockingbear's words when I'd told him of my decision: "Be careful what you ask for," he said. "This is especially important when requesting ceremony." He'd also added, "I expect your life will be shaken up a bit." I didn't ask what he meant.

Just two days after offering tobacco to Shirley, at my annual health checkup, my doctor found two breast lumps that needed further examination. It was unsettling news. A mammogram was ordered, and during the week's wait for the appointment, I began hearing a small but clear voice telling me not to be concerned. Could I trust the voice? Was my mind making this up in an effort to calm myself? It didn't feel that way; the inner voice was filled with clarity and truth. I did my best to keep my mind occupied and focused on trusting my intuition.

The mammogram revealed the lumps as benign. I was relieved, and also aware that the inner work of my quest had something to do with trusting inner guidance.

Preparation for quest included making prayer ties. Each morning from the day I presented tobacco until the day of my quest, I rose early to pray. Beside me sat a basket filled with tobacco, a roll of string, and cotton fabric swatches I'd cut into two-inch squares, in colors corresponding to each of the seven sacred directions: East, South, West, North, Father Sky, Mother Earth, and Spirit Within. As I prayed to each direction, I wrapped a pinch of tobacco in a square of fabric, gathered the corners together, and pulled a section of the long string around the corners to close the tiny prayer package. Each prayer was an offering of highest intention and gratitude to the spirits of that direction in exchange for their blessings. This long string of prayers would become my circle of protection during the quest. Every day, for five months, I connected seven tiny tobacco bundles to one long string and wound them onto a stick. As time passed, my prayers deepened and the bundle of prayer ties thickened. The final bundle was composed of nearly eleven hundred multicolored offerings.

During the months preparing for quest, I struggled to make another doll. Embarking on quest, I thought, should coincide with creating the doll of the north. In Rockingbear's circle, I'd learned that the north direction of the medicine wheel relates to elderhood and correlates to the archetype of the warrior. In the healing doll journey, the north symbolizes identifying the gifts that emerge from your woundedness and experiencing a renewed sense of wholeness. While *Fear*, my scapegoat or shadow doll, had appeared in the south, the doll of the north would represent the antithesis of *Fear's* painful emotion. It would stand as an image of power; it would be my talisman. This doll would pull me out of my past and into a strengthened present and future. I was certain it would share teachings about self-trust and acceptance of the unfolding perfection of life.

Partway through construction of the doll, I carefully held its clay arms in an upright position, bent the wire armature that defined the doll's posture, and wedged the clay into the fiber shoulder sockets, hoping this would keep her arms extended high above her head in an expression of victory. The doll's construction had been a challenge. The first face I sculpted had a grossly misshapen nose, and I had to remake the head entirely. As well, her hair wasn't what I envisioned; it was thin and stringy rather than rich and full-bodied. The arms were just another structural defect that kept the doll from being complete. I was frustrated but wasn't going to give up.

In just three weeks, I'd go up the mountain for four days and nights without food or water. I looked forward to being alone in nature, growing closer to Spirit in prayer and gratitude. My willingness to be challenged on this quest felt perfectly timed with the arrival of the doll of the north.

Had I been paying attention, I would've felt my resistance. But I wasn't listening—or didn't want to. I was intent on finishing the doll. She symbolized fulfillment of the dreams I'd held for myself. Wholeness felt imminent, and I envisioned being fully healed, living a life free of pain and filled with purpose and inspiration.

But this was a head game, a story I'd played into multiple times. In retrospect, there were clear signs letting me know the timing wasn't right for my talisman to arrive. The doll's problematic construction mimicked my own aggrieved body, and my struggle with her showed me I was forcing the process. Once I realized my overzealousness, the doll was nearly done, so I completed her and gave her to Sharon as a thank-you for supporting me in her women's circle.

Days after receiving the gift, Sharon called to let me know the doll's arms had fallen to her sides. *No victory yet,* I thought. *Just another indicator that I'm pushing my process.* I repaired Sharon's doll as best I could and chose to step back from doll making for the near future. I made a vow that listening would take precedence—my feeling sense would take priority over my thoughts. And I would no longer sit in quiet and call in more dolls; I told the doll spirits that I would wait for them to call me. They would need to be loud to get my attention.

I hadn't even stepped foot on the mountain, and I'd already encountered important lessons about trusting my inner voice and not pushing to make things happen. With quest less than two weeks away, I felt my anxiety rise, but not for reasons that might seem obvious: the darkness, the unknown, being alone outdoors without food and water. I was afraid I wouldn't hear Spirit's message. My concept of a vision was akin to the sky opening up, a beam of light descending, angels with trumpets, and a loud voice revealing some enlightened truth. I knew it wouldn't happen that way, but I wished it would. I wanted the assurance I'd "get it," that I'd receive and understand this coveted guidance. I didn't yet trust that I had all the awareness I needed.

A Fierce Belief in Miracles

Ten days before quest, a boil the size of a golf ball rose up directly between my eyebrows. I'd never had an abscess, and this one definitely had my attention. While it was painful and distressing, it also felt prophetic. *Perhaps*, I thought, *this is a sign I'm creating an opening for what's to come.* At a walk-in clinic I learned how to clean, bandage, and care for the boil while on my quest, and it did begin to recede slightly, but it was clear I would take this physical messenger up the mountain as a reminder that I was aptly prepared to tune in to any messages from Spirit. The afternoon prior to leaving for quest, a cashier in a health food store took one look at me and said, "I see your third eye is opening." She wished me well. It felt like a confirmation: the way had been paved for me to receive a vision; I needn't be concerned. And the boil would heal itself. *Trust.*

On the day quest began, the community was up before dawn. We had stayed in nearby cabins the night before so we could be together at sunrise. I gathered my few belongings into my backpack—a tarp, some rope, a knife, toiletries in plastic bags, a fleece pullover, rain gear, and my prayer ties—and met Shirley and others by the fire. As the sun began to peek over the mountain, a circle sister escorted me to my questing spot, which was marked by several strips of red cotton tied to some low-hanging maple limbs at the crest of a hill.

I carefully unwound my long string of prayer ties. A screech owl sounded in the distant forest. Tiny spots of color splattered across the forest floor as the long string of colored prayer packets were stretched out to encircle my questing spot; they jumped from the carpet of leaves to the branches of saplings and back down again. I attached a small tarp to some trees inside the circle of prayers to provide me shelter from rain. Then I settled myself in a comfortable spot on the edge of a hillside and became quiet.

Commitment

Six other sisters quested with me that year, all tucked along the sides of the mountain, circled by their prayers.

My first two days of quest were frustrating. I sat quietly, the only exception being a mass of hoverflies that continuously buzzed around me. Often confused with wasps or bees, hoverflies are large striped pollinators that have the ability to hover in one place—in my quest experience, directly in front of one's face—while incessantly buzzing. I swatted at them and moved to different spots, hoping to evade them, to no avail. It was late afternoon of day two when I realized I might ask the hoverflies what they had come to teach me. So, I placed myself directly among a tiny swarm of the creatures and put forth the question: "Do you have something to share with me?"

The answer was immediate. "We're here to distract you because we know how much you enjoy that."

I didn't like their answer; it angered me. I also knew it was true.

"Okay, I got it," I replied. "Starting now, I'm choosing to have no distractions so I can hear what I need to hear and feel what I need to feel." I was sincere in wanting to focus on being present.

Within the hour, the hoverflies disappeared, not to return for the rest of my stay. Instead, a variety of other messengers appeared: a large toad, distant flute music, the soil beneath me, a tall oak, the sun, and the moon. I held conversations with them all, newly aware of their beautiful language and the compelling wisdom of their messages.

So this is how it's done, I thought. *I just need to be still, eliminate distraction, pay attention, and take it all in.* No clouds parting, no blaring trumpets or angels. Just simply being, listening. I knew how to do this.

Going without food and water was not as daunting as I expected. The community at the fire was eating and drinking for each of the questers, and I rarely felt hungry. I occasionally got thirsty. At those times, I took the advice Shirley had given me and sucked on a small stone to create saliva in my dry mouth. I also became chilled at times and would layer every bit of clothing I'd brought with me. Those by the fire later told me that my representative stone in their circle often felt cold to the touch; they'd kept it near the fire for most of the quest.

As the sun set on my second day, beautiful Native flute music drifted up the mountain. I slumbered a little and woke to the moonlight. After the quest I asked who in the community had shared this calming melody and was told there had been no flute music by the fire. "That was Spirit helping you settle in," Shirley said.

As I sat alone on top of the mountain, my perceptions were both heightened and profound. The exchange of information and emotion with all beings and life itself felt natural and rich and illuminating. As I expanded my perceptions, I was able to discern my unique way of interpreting the whispers of the wind, the feel of the earth beneath my feet, and the touch of rain on my skin. There were parts of my experience that humored me and others that brought tears. It was in this manner that Spirit spoke to and through me. All that was required of me was to listen. My trust in myself and in Spirit was renewed.

On the evening of day three, I felt complete. Grounded in my connection with Spirit, I felt confident I had received my vision. I offered gratitudes to all of my relations—to my grandmothers, to the spirits of the land, to the women who tended the quest fire and fed the community, and to my fellow questers who sat in prayer on the mountain. I tenderly rolled up my tarp and prayer ties and hiked down the mountain.

Two sisters greeted me with bowed heads, relieved me of my pack, and guided me to the fire. I thanked the flames and my relations for their support and protection. Then I set my bundle of prayer ties into the fire where it briefly glowed, then withered, my prayers being carried by smoke to the heavens.

Shirley took me into the sweat lodge and invited me to lie on the earth. Another woman brought me chilled hibiscus tea from the kitchen. It was the first liquid I'd had in nearly four days and the best thing I'd ever tasted.

23

Talisman

Not quite two years after quest, something shifted. Though my hips had given me trouble for years, this felt different. There was a stabbing pain in my left hip that traveled down the length of the leg. In order to walk, I needed to pull myself up from a sitting position, grip my left thigh, and adjust its position in the joint—a painful endeavor. I relied on a cane to walk. Though the pain and hassle of moving caused me to stay still as much as possible, I continued to facilitate women's circles and healing work out of my home. This kept me connected with community and gave me a sense of value and purpose.

Through Internet research I accurately diagnosed that I had a labral tear—a split in the cartilage of my left hip joint. I was intent on taking the least invasive approach to fix the problem and found a local surgeon who could repair the cartilage via laparoscopic surgery. This way I would avoid the alternative of hip replacement.

But six months after the surgery, my hip was still sore and not fully supporting my weight. The surgeon encouraged me to continue strengthening, so I joined a gym for twice-weekly visits with a personal coach. The pain of this work was excruciating, and I often broke into tears before my hour-long session was complete.

I was as frustrated as I was pained. Walking on crutches, unable to place full weight on my left hip for a couple of months, the circulation in that leg diminished, and the skin on my foot and calf began turning gray. Tom and my parents were pressuring me to have the hip replaced. The combination of pain and resistance turned into anger and depression. I struggled to focus on anything positive. The downward spiral became a strain on me and my family. Eventually all the suggestions and frustrations melded into complete overwhelm. At that point, having descended into spiritual darkness, I sought the support of a local intuitive astrologer. I had little knowledge of astrology but welcomed any divine communication that might provide light.

It was early fall of 2013 when Liz and I met at her home. Crutches in hand and holding tightly to the rail, I climbed the steps to her second-floor studio. The room felt light and inviting, high windows spilling sunshine through prisms and casting rainbows on walls and across our knees as we sat facing one another. I'd sent Liz my birth information before our session so she could prepare my astrological chart.

After opening our session with a brief prayer, Liz pointed out the themes in my chart. "You're Sagittarius rising, which means Jupiter is the ruling planet of your entire chart. Jupiter rules the hips, a greater search for meaning, and forward momentum. The south node is in Capricorn, which rules bone structure. So, you came into this life with a predisposition to structure and to life being hard."

I was intrigued that she knew so much about me from a chart of lines and symbols based only on the date and time I was born.

"Yes, it's felt like healing has been a full-time job for me," I said.

"That makes sense. Your chart shows that for years your healing has been a demand that feels beyond reason. Part of what you're being asked to heal now is in your emotional realm."

"I've already done that," I said emphatically. "Is there something more I need to address?"

"There's been a theme around not listening to your own wisdom about how to move forward. It's really important for you to feel into the choices you make, to not use your logical mind."

"Are there steps you recommend to guide me?"

"Well, it's not so clear-cut," Liz said. "The quality of surrender you need to have may feel like you're going through a death and a birth at the same time. What I hear intuitively is 'your will has been broken.'"

Her words made sense. I had done all I could to heal myself emotionally and spiritually. What I resisted was another surgery—not just any surgery, but one that involved cutting off the top of the femur. It felt intrusive and beyond what I had the energy to cope with. But there didn't seem to be any option except to surrender. I would have no control over the outcome. *Would I be able to walk again? Would I end up in a wheelchair?* I felt frightened and confused.

"Do you have suggestions for how best to approach this?" I asked.

"The great thing about this process of surrender is that with the influence of Pisces in your chart, you'll be malleable."

"Malleable feels like a good quality, but I'd also really groove on some clarity and direction," I said with a smirk.

Liz chuckled. "Here's the thing. You're very intuitive and very bright. It's important that you take everything you've learned into consideration and then do what *feels* right to you in the moment—like being in a dark room and feeling your way along the walls in order to find an opening or a doorway. You're in uncharted territory."

"Uncharted territory" was an apt description, and though I wanted a map, I felt a tad comforted to know I was on the right track in simply feeling as lost as I did. In my mind, I felt committed to exploring this uncharted territory, though I didn't like how it felt at that moment. I reminded myself that I was being asked to listen, act, and trust—just as I'd learned to do on the firewalk and on quest. *I can do this.*

Just days after my visit with Liz, the image of a doll came to me in a dream. The next morning I sculpted its body out of wire and began journaling with it, asking what colors and textures best represented its form. The doll wanted to be wrapped in brightly colored fabric with sparkly beads strewn over its torso and limbs. A few days later, its face became clear in my vision, and I worked with clay on a Styrofoam egg to create what I saw in my mind's eye—an expression of surprise.

The doll then requested that I wrap it in black-and-white fabric. This felt troubling to me. I didn't want to cover up the multicolored, vibrant body I'd spent so much time creating. But since listening and allowing were my priorities, I did as the doll asked. I cut half-inch strips of checkered black-and-white fabric and carefully bound parts of the doll's torso and appendages, leaving the ends of the fabric strip in the doll's hands. The head still had no hair; in fact, the back of the head was an exposed Styrofoam egg. The doll then told me it was complete, and its name was *Unraveling of the Black and White.*

I felt resistance, wanting to remove the black-and-white fabric to reveal the underlying radiance originally requested, to finish the head with a proper hairdo. When I journaled with it, *Unraveling* revealed a message I've remembered for years: "The present moment holds our completeness. There are always layers to peel away, parts we'd like to change or embellish. Sometimes this present moment doesn't look or feel 'pretty.' There's a creative, colorful way to live, but you can't judge something and, at the same time, perceive its wholeness. Letting go of your rules will reveal the wonder and beauty in each moment."

I was struck with the directness of this wisdom. I had covered up life's color and novelty with my desire for order and control, my own perception of what "should" be. I kept *Unraveling* displayed on a side table in my healing space for months as a reminder of her valuable teaching.

In my Healing Touch practice, I began to view my sessions as another way to *feel* my way through uncharted territory. My dolls, several of which were displayed in my healing space, had grown increasingly vocal during sessions, and I acknowledged them regularly.

Many of my clients were women who had experienced sexual trauma. Addressing sensitive issues around trauma came easily to me, and the dolls were often integral to this process. Listening to their whispered messages during a session, I gained clarity on a client's deeper issues and was often given words or methods that would help individuals better understand themselves. The dolls spoke to me only if their message was pertinent to the client, so I never felt distracted when they nudged me for attention. Their work and mine seemed to weave together in a synchronistic way. If a client felt anxiety, for example, *Fear* would ask me to move energy in a particular way or ask that I share some words with the client. If a client tended to be intellectual or heady, *Unraveling* often asked me to suggest creative practices or a meditation that focused on allowing. *Compassionate Mother* often encouraged words about self-care, being gentle with one-self, and asking for help.

When I spoke with clients before and after their sessions, any messages I needed to share came from deep within me, much like the whispers of the dolls. Listening carefully, I waited for the nudge of rich warm energy that rose up from my belly and wanted to speak. I rarely told clients where these messages came from, but they were inevitably received with acknowledg-ment, gratitude, and sometimes tears. I was learning what Liz had tried to explain to me. I carefully felt my way along unfa-miliar passages, listened for inner nudges, and sensed when and where to alter course. I began silently thanking the dolls in advance of a healing session, knowing they were helping me as much as they helped my clients.

Later in the fall of 2013, a new doll began to take form. The spirit of the doll felt strongly feminine, and she pulled on my attention day and night until I finally focused my hands on cre-ating her. I'd felt her hovering in the ether for nearly four years. In fact, I'd occasionally sketched parts of her—a form or a face—and played with her colors on watercolor paper. But I hadn't wanted to push her process and was delighted when she began to prod me more forcefully.

She was created from the same fabric as my false talis-man—a batiked indigo cotton printed with lovely golden star symbols. The newly forming doll also had arms extending over her head, but this time her figure was powerful and robust; she held great strength in her armature and her arms. She rose from fiber flames; she had copper-and gold-ribboned full-bodied hair, and metallic gold highlights painted on her face. In her hands she held a drum and a beating stick. She named herself *She Who Drums*. Her vibrant energy felt promising in the midst of painful days. Her presence alone encouraged me to take inventory of my gifts—including those she termed "hidden gifts." It was time, she said, to identify the gifts I'd been given, to view them as strengths, and to carry them confidently and openly into the world. One morning as I journaled with her, she shared this poem:

Beat Your Drum

You did not come here to be silent
You were called to beat your drum

Your drum
Your medicine

There is no other here at this time
Who brings what you bring

Come
Come from the shadows
Circle 'round this fire
Weave your blanket among us

And sing your song
Pound your feet upon the earth
Be witnessed

It is *your* drum the people await
Your drum that completes us

Your drum inspires the dream
Heals the wound
Transforms the moment

This moment
Now

You did not come here to be silent
It is time to beat your drum

The doll's powerful presence and encouragement, however, seemed mismatched with my physical condition. I was still strengthening with weights, but outside the gym I was walking on crutches. It had been two years since the surgery to repair the torn cartilage, and I was losing confidence that I would ever be able to walk with strength and ease. *She Who Drums* arrived with perfect timing, giving me the hope I needed. Her invitation to "beat my drum" reminded me that I wouldn't be called without the ability to respond.

I didn't know how I would find the fortitude and vitality to bring my gifts to others, but the doll's uplifting spirit resonated with a seed of faith deep within me that I'd been nurturing for years. *She Who Drums* became the catalyst for a healing transformation that was soon to deliver me from the ashes.

24

Painbody

E ew! This makes me feel yucky inside," Joseph exclaimed as he gingerly plucked my newest doll from its hiding place behind the computer monitor. It made me feel yucky, too, which is why I hid it. *Painbody* was composed of clay; its two stumpy leg bones were wired haphazardly to a black pelvis, which was pierced through the left hip joint with a bent nail. Red clay surrounded the site of the "injury." The doll's head, which sat directly atop its pelvis, was gruesome, its neck pulling away from the injured joint, its eyes bulging from its pale face, its mouth gaping in misery.

A week prior, I was working out at the gym, suffering through my second set of back squats, when *Painbody* came to me in a vision. Lifting weights had become some of the most painful work I'd entrusted myself to, but in pursuit of healing, I felt it was worth the agony.

Painbody barged into my awareness that day with such clarity and insistence that I ended my workout early, drove home, and pulled out my clay to bring the doll into form. I was surprised by the intensity of her debut. Her urgent introduction meant she had a message, and I was intent on making her while the vision was clear and strong.

The doll was creepy, and I felt embarrassed by her. Many quiet mornings, I pulled the doll from her hiding spot and connected with her through journaling. I was quick to tuck her away when I was done. She was visually repulsive, and explaining why I'd created this hideous figure was a conversation I preferred to avoid.

I tried to stay curious, but I felt unsettled in the doll's presence. Our first dialogue surprised me. Instead of my usual questioning, I found myself directing anger toward her about all the ways the pain she represented had disrupted my life. And I didn't like her responses, which I knew on some level were true and just pushed me further into resistance. So I looked for common ground, a starting place where I would be less reactive and more receptive.

In these journaling sessions, *Painbody* had plenty to share. She told me that my body held as much ease as pain; I'd just chosen to focus on pain. *Hmmm. Why had I not considered focusing on ease?* She also noted that ease of movement comes from allowing sensation to *move*, not focusing on where it's *stuck*. I learned that my resistance was a pattern I'd developed from years of avoiding freedom, because freedom held the possibility of being harmed. *What did the path of ease look like?* I asked myself.

A thought popped into my head that ease might look like surgery, but I quickly reconsidered. No, I wanted to heal naturally, from the inside out. *Painbody* gently challenged me on that judgment.

"Your insistence on natural nonsurgical healing has resulted in your current level of health. You can't continue on this course and arrive at a different result. To find a new level of health, you'll need to let go of your judgment."

A Fierce Belief in Miracles

Though I'd received other teachings about judgment, this one touched me in a new way. I realized that the rigidness in my body was likely mirroring my obstinance about natural healing. I felt a small chink in my armor; my body relaxed into the thought that being receptive might produce a new outcome—relief, I hoped.

What happened over the next several days was remarkable. The pain I'd held for years shifted. It no longer showed up as a nerve-pinching, gut-wrenching, fall-to-my-knees sensation. Instead, my body simply felt sore, and I felt tired. With this change, *Painbody* directed me to alter my exercise from weight-lifting to gentle movement in a warm pool. The pool was a welcome respite from the gym, and over the next several weeks my body relaxed into nurturing warm water and appreciated gentler movement and the sensation of being buoyant.

After that dialogue, I kept *Painbody* on my desk in plain view. My anger toward her transformed into appreciation, even respect. One winter morning after weeks without conversing, *Painbody* suddenly demanded my attention.

"It's time," *Painbody* announced as I placed a log on the remaining coals in our wood stove.

"Time for what?" I asked.

"I want you to remove the nail from my hip."

"Why?"

"It no longer needs to be there."

Though curious, I didn't continue our dialogue but began to consider the steps required to remove the nail. It wasn't a simple task. The nail was large and bent at a right angle where it pierced the pelvis. The doll was made of polymer clay that had been baked with the bent nail already inserted. The pelvis wasn't pliable, and there was no simple way for the nail to be removed. I asked Tom how I could extract it without destroying the doll.

He promptly suggested sawing the nail just near the joint so that it could be easily removed. It sounded like the best option for success, and I set a time for us to work on it together.

That evening I took *Painbody* to the basement, along with a candle and some sage. A change as drastic as this was clearly a moment for ceremony. Tom pulled out his Dremel tool and attached a cutoff blade as I secured *Painbody's* pelvis in the bench clamp and smudged the area with sage.

"Creator, I call on you, on my angels and guides, and on all benevolent spirits to assist me in receiving with clarity and understanding any messages that are important for me to hear at this time. I ask that the removal of this nail from *Painbody* be done with ease and comfort."

While I monitored the clamp and angle of the doll's body, Tom carefully sawed through the nail. I caught the two pieces as they fell and held them in the palm of my hand. I thanked Tom for his help and he went back to his office, then I took some gauze and gently wrapped the wounded pelvis as if the doll had just finished a surgical procedure. As I tended to *Painbody*, she spoke.

"It's time for you to call a surgeon."

My breath caught. I knew she was referring to my own need for surgery.

"Why did you wait until now to tell me this?" I asked.

"Because you were so intense and resistant a few months ago. You needed time to loosen up, to become open to the possibility that a second surgery could help you."

Tears welled in my eyes. I knew how fearful I was of surgery. Spending time with *Painbody* had been a way of introducing me to the idea, and exercising in the warm pool was a way to soften my spirit. *Painbody* helped me understand that I needn't suffer any longer; there was a way to experience relief and comfort, even strength.

The following day, I scheduled an appointment with an orthopedic surgeon. It was a date long overdue.

I removed the cloth hospital gown and put my clothes on. Tom and I waited for the doctor. Soon the door opened, and Dr. K snapped the X-ray onto the viewing screen.

"What do you think we should do?" he asked.

I looked at the picture. The head of my left femur was half an inch outside of its socket. No wonder I'd been hurting so miserably. In that moment, I let go of my doubts and hesitations about having my hip replaced. It suddenly seemed the most practical path to healing.

"When can I schedule surgery?" I asked.

Just hours before, I had been considering the next steps in my strength conditioning routine. But Dr. K was fully confident that replacing the hip would transform my pain and I would be walking without crutches or discomfort in six to eight months. Dr. K was known for his expertise in this type of surgery, and with his assurance, I finally felt true relief and hope. Before I left the office, I had set a date for total hip replacement surgery: June 2, 2014.

25

Seed

In some respects, June 2 could not have arrived soon enough. I cringed just thinking of the image on the X-ray, and I felt certain that surgery was my best chance at ever walking normally again. Still, I was hesitant as the date approached. Part of my anxiety was the inherent risk of the procedure, but I had a deeper concern. I'd been in physical pain for nearly twenty-five years. Change was imminent, and there was no guarantee of the outcome.

Through years of healing, I'd learned that physical symptoms that originated from emotional wounds could be treated and seemingly cured, only to reappear as some new symptom. I associated the pain in my pelvis and hips with being raped. The wound was deep-seated and visceral. I'd explored my grief and trauma through dozens of methods. My self-examination had felt thorough, illuminating debilitating patterns and untrue beliefs, addressing them as best I could. Still, the thought of having surgery and then experiencing more pain of whatever description made me feel nauseated.

I've done all I can do to heal this issue, I told myself. *Having my hip replaced is the last step in the process.* So many times I'd engaged in wishful thinking, only to find I'd convinced myself that things should be other than what they actually were. I feared the disappointment of facing another chapter of painful searching. More than anything, I wanted the freedom to move comfortably. *Freedom.* My prayer was for freedom.

Two days after surgery, even though the swelling had not subsided, it was much easier to move my left hip in multiple directions. Placing weight on my leg felt stable. Turning in bed no longer produced piercing pain. The newfound support in my physical body gave me a clarity and confidence I hadn't felt in years. Within a week after my return home, the change felt so dramatic I called the doctor's office and scheduled a second surgery, this time to replace my right hip.

Within a span of six months, both hips were replaced. It was as if my body had been a bike with two flat tires that had just been patched and inflated. One moment, the ride was harsh and slow going; the next, it had transformed into steady, smooth movement. I felt the same excitement I'd felt as a young girl learning to ride my bicycle.

The transformation went beyond the physical. That I was suddenly pain-free and walking with strength was a miracle. While it took only days for the pain of surgery to subside, it took months to process my emotions about it. I was in disbelief that this was my same body, albeit with some alterations. I could squat to pick up something on the ground. I could walk with confident strides. I could put on my socks. I could kick a ball. For over twenty years, I'd longed for freedom, and now I embodied it. The feeling was extraordinary. Intent on treating my body with great care and consideration, I carefully and gently resumed activity, amazed at my new abilities and at the sweetness of ease and comfort in my hips.

Seed

That fall, I acquired a frisky white golden retriever puppy, eight weeks old. Slow and steady, Szoke and I began hiking the trails near our home. Our walks—at first a strengthening regimen—became and remain a daily ritual, a time to appreciate the miracle of movement, of nature, of breath.

In the fall of 2016, I received a call from the local rape crisis center, inviting me to be the featured artist in their annual Survivor Art Show, a venue for survivors of sexual violence to exhibit their creative work. I felt honored to show my work and excited for the dolls' messages to be shared.

I was working on a new doll at the time. She had been coming along slowly, and I enjoyed the gentle way she was presenting herself. As I prepared my other dolls for the show, she prodded me to complete her. It was clear she wanted to take part in the show. Carefully, with her whispered guidance, I created her body upright and attentive, dressed her in batiked fabric dyed deep red and bronze. She emerged as an elder with a warm smile and wise bright eyes. Her face was captivating with soft white hair highlighting golden skin and glowing cheeks, her expression knowing and curious. I had journaled with her briefly and knew she had an affinity for seeds. Her name, she told me, was *Going to Seed*.

My first thought was of dandelions. I was reminded of my childhood, of the many prayers and wishes I'd sent out on dandelion fluff. I smiled remembering how those youthful moments of prayer had always been more memorable than any of the outcomes. Working with various beads and thread, I attempted to replicate delicate dandelion seeds, but try as I might, I couldn't find a way to make them. It was obvious this was not the seed she wanted. I decided to give it a day or two and then return to the project with a clear mind and heart.

A Fierce Belief in Miracles

It was a sunny fall morning a couple of days after my failed dandelion attempts. I sat with the nearly completed doll. Her face and hands, made of clay, were hardened and painted, her fabric bodice and hair intact. She awaited her seeds. I decided to engage with her through dominant/non-dominant handwriting.

"What did you come to share?" I asked. Her words came quickly and with clarity.

"I'm here to represent the stage of life when one's gifts are concentrated and ready to disperse to the larger world."

"And what type of seed would best express this?"

"One with vigor and vitality, one that's long-lasting," she said.

I immediately thought of the lotus flower and its dried seed-pods. My mother had collected them and used them in flower arrangements and on wreaths. I'd been fascinated with the lotus's large circular pod and the unusual way the seeds nested, each in its own hole.

I researched the lotus and learned the seeds can remain viable for centuries. Medicinally, they're used for restoring vital force in the body and nourishing jing, the essence of life. Lotus seeds are carried by water, an element associated with emotion. The lotus flower emerges from muddy waters unspoiled and pure and is a symbol of wise and spiritually enlightened qualities in a person—a perfect fit for this wise elder doll.

Lastly, I learned that the lotus plant is associated with rebirth and faith. A magazine article on the lotus plant by freelance writer Katie Robinson caught my attention: "Not only does [the lotus] find sanctuary in the muck, but due to the waxy protection layer on its petals, its beauty is blithely unaffected when it re-blooms each morning. It continues to resurrect itself, coming back just as beautiful as it was last seen. With such refusal to accept defeat, it's almost impossible not to associate this flower with unwavering faith."

Seed

Unwavering faith, I thought. *Perfect.*

With some searching, I acquired a dried lotus pod with seeds still in it. The stem of the pod fit perfectly in the doll's right hand, like a rod or staff. I painted the seeds within each hole a luminous golden color. Removing one of them, I placed it in the palm of the doll's left hand—an offering to others. The seeds remaining in the pod await their time to be planted.

26

Prayer

On a late fall morning in 2017, the sun had been up for only an hour, its light penetrating the branches of oaks and pines that lined the parkway and sprinkling across the pavement. With smooth roads ahead and the sun rising before me, I pedaled slowly, meditatively, the morning's breeze cooling me. Being back on my bike felt exhilarating. It was akin to tasting my first liquids after quest; I didn't realize how refreshing it would be.

In the three years since my hips had been replaced, I hadn't felt inspired to get on the bike. My body had limped and compensated for such a long time that, with new joints, I'd felt more comfortable with my feet on the ground, hiking and walking to regain balance and stamina.

But that morning, my bike had called me to ride. I dusted off its frame, inflated its tires, lubricated its chain, and replaced the rear flasher battery. This attention was long overdue. For years, the bike had been my close companion. When life became turbulent, riding its saddle had been my respite—a place where I could experience the ease of turning pedals on a long, smooth straightaway; where coasting downhill swept troubles and anxiety behind me; where I could more easily connect with inner strength and full-hearted joy.

I sensed that the bike had a message for me as I headed out on the ride. Cycling often inspired a flow of words; I'd composed many poems while gliding along area roadways. And I'd woken up that morning, thinking about writing a book. I'd long intended to put words to my story some day. I imagined sharing it with readers who'd been through circumstances similar to mine, and assuring them it wasn't unreasonable to hold faith for a bright outcome.

For years after being raped, I'd scoured library shelves and later the Internet, searching for a true and uplifting account of someone who had healed from rape. I longed to read a story that offered a fresh perspective and hope for my own future. I discovered a handful of personal stories that offered insight into maladies associated with post-traumatic stress and the hardship faced by survivors of sexual violence. But none offered me hope as I confronted the daunting task of healing my body, emotions, and spirit. Though I'd felt inspired to write a book after my case went to court, I'd postponed committing to the work. Mending body and emotions had required more attention than anticipated, and not having healed myself, I believed my story would offer little hope to others.

As I'd prepared for the day's ride I'd felt hesitant—even a little resistant. Getting my bike out the door had required a good deal of self-encouragement. I'd rallied myself with visions of coasting along the scenic parkway and the feeling of inner strength that always followed a ride. Despite its many joys, cycling is filled with challenges: steep ascents, rough pavement, passing cars, dark tunnels, and roads through unfamiliar territory. I didn't feel as steady and comfortable in my saddle as the last time I rode, and I decided to not push so hard on steep climbs and take extra care on descents.

As I pedaled slowly along, I reflected on how my work had evolved in the three years since I'd been on the bike. Once I'd recovered from surgery, I began doing more of the work that inspired me most, paying attention to how experiences felt emotionally. I began attracting more Healing Touch clients and facilitating circles for girls and women, providing space for them to honor their emotions and speak their truth. I offered empowerment workshops for girls and their mothers, and I shared my healing dolls by offering talks to local organizations interested in stories of healing or art as therapy. Over time, I felt noticeably stronger and more confident—that morning, enough so to get back on the bike.

The sun had risen above the treetops and was feeling warm on my shoulders. I approached the first ascent—a steep one—and geared down, pushing pedals with a slow, steady rhythm as I crept toward the crest of the hill. I felt no pain, and my lungs took in the fresh mountain air. I coasted a section of parkway shaded from the sun and slowed my pace, breathing in ease of movement, breathing out gratitude.

I turned onto a short gravel descent leading to a paved road nicely shaded by rhododendron and hardwoods. I wasn't sure where the road would lead or what challenges I'd face, but in that moment I knew my prayers for ease and wholeness in my life, for passion and faith had been answered, and I wanted to be fully present in a moment of appreciation for those gifts. I attuned to the quiet beauty of passing trees, the air brushing my bare skin, my legs and breath finding their cadence, the delight of it all.

I suddenly felt a sense of déjà vu. For the past twenty years, I had held a clear intention and vision of riding just like this—moving with ease, full of joy, feeling a sense of direction and purpose in life. My heart swelled.

As I reflected on the wonder of the moment, I realized my most important work—what I now call "heart work"—is ceremonial prayer and intention. For nearly two decades, I'd made prayer and intention a spiritual practice. Commemorating life transitions, visioning the future, blessing people and spaces, offering prayers for healing, expressing gratitude—all these actions felt satisfying and rewarding, and I had incorporated them naturally into my healing and facilitation work. *Thank you, Spirit, for this incredibly beautiful moment.*

Turns out my bike did have a message for me that day. As I coasted in the sunshine down a long, smooth stretch of road, I heard a clear voice that it was time for me to write.

"Write what?" I asked.

"Your story," the voice replied.

My stomach turned as chills ran up my arms—a familiar sensation of excitement and fear. "I'm not ready," I said. "I'm not sure how my story will end. Nor even how it will begin."

"Ceremony," I heard.

"Yes, the perfect beginning," I said.

When I returned home, I contacted friends from my Earth Green circle and requested them to prepare ceremony for me. I asked that it take place on the water. "My intention is flow," I told them. "It's time to write."

It was a Saturday in February of 2018. Three women friends from Earth Green circle met me on the banks of the Ivy River north of Asheville. We'd gathered for tea earlier in the month to share our visions of what a ceremony for "flow" could look like. Originally, we'd planned to meet at a pond, but two days before ceremony, I woke from a dream of flowing waters and knew the water for ceremony needed movement, as in a stream or river. I called a friend to ask if we could do ceremony on her land next to the Ivy River. She agreed at once.

The day was partly cloudy with a chill in the air. I'd worn my bathing suit under a skirt and T-shirt as I knew I'd be getting wet. The four of us hiked to the river's edge. There we removed our shoes, our toes meeting the soft sand that was slightly warmed by the noonday sun. Together we set an altar, exchanged words of love and support, and began our ceremony with drumming and prayer. Elana and I walked into the fast-moving river, the slippery stones requiring attentive steps. My feet and lower legs were quickly numbed by the frigid waters, yet my emotional sensitivity was heightened.

As Elana spoke to each direction, she dipped a colored strip of cotton fabric in water, praying aloud for the spirits of that direction to support my intention. Her words were followed by my own silent prayers, and Elana brought the soaked cloth above my head, twisting along its length to wring out the water as it anointed me. The cool air against my wet skin caused shivers that seemed to cast off any fear or resistance I'd held. Like moss detaching from river rocks, my resistance slipped away in the rapidly moving waters, drifted downstream and out of sight.

When all the directions had been honored with prayer, I walked into the center of the river, its waters rising on my bare thighs. I stood for long minutes looking downstream, tears dripping on already wet cheeks, whispering words of gratitude to the river, to Spirit, to the land, and to the moment. Then I submerged myself. Allowing the river to do its final cleansing, I released any self-doubt or inhibitions about writing into the fast-flowing water.

Back on the banks of the river, I grabbed my towel and dried my body, then changed into dry clothing. The four of us sat in

Prayer

silence watching the clouds and river drift by. We shared a small feast we'd brought—some homemade zucchini bread, nuts, and turmeric milk. And we shared gifts of gratitude with one another. I felt ready for my next steps.

At home, I sat at my desk before sunrise, the windows still dark.

"Where shall I begin?" I asked the gentle spirits surrounding me and the dolls gathered in my space.

Their response was a chorus of clarity and direction.

"With prayer."

Acknowledgments

To my husband, Tom, for his encouragement and support through long days of writing and rewriting. Thank you for holding the vision of this book with me.

Putting my experience into words has been challenging, and I'm deeply indebted to friends who offered wise reflection and suggestions for improving my work. This was immensely helpful. The loving and gracious ways you responded and offered feedback didn't go unnoticed. Big hugs and gratitude to Jan Beauregard, Barbara Brady, Susan Gale, Glenn Geffcken, Maria Geffcken, Julie Heck, Mel Kelly, Ann Kraybill, Jackie Kuhn, Elise Lasko, Judy Ray, Lisa Rough, Elizabeth Schussler, Jill Scobie, Cathy Scott, and Jinny Wallerstedt.

There are numerous practitioners and angels who've graced my path over the years, offering one or many teachings, exercises, meditations, suggestions, and gentle invitations for me to alter course, to know myself more clearly, to dig deeper, to laugh louder, to let go, to allow, to have faith, and to trust myself. I apologize in advance for those whom I will likely and unintentionally omit. A gracious thanks to Will Rockingbear, for the clear and loving way you taught me, and for the repeated reminder to trust myself. To Sharon, for modeling the beautiful path of self-compassion; to Shirley, for seeing the healer in me and for watching my back as I quested on the mountain; to Dr. Pat, for your self-assured way of addressing my imbalances and for teaching me to pay attention to life's signs and symbols; to Joey, who taught me the undeniable power of blessings; to Dr. Nabors, who, in addition to your commitment to provide care and comfort in the dentist chair, made time and effort to understand and support my journey; to Dr. K, whose assurance, presence, and compassion helped me step toward the possibility of titanium hips and relearning how to walk with strength in this world; to Barb Kobe, for mentoring me in the healing art of doll making and for your enthusiastic support of me sharing this story. Immense thanks to my incredible writing coach and editor, Darlene Frank. You've been my steady, offering practical tips and heartfelt encouragement. I'm grateful for the beautiful way you do your work.

About the Author

photo credit: Sheila Mraz

Anne Heck's life work is devoted to inspiring and guiding others to trust themselves, open to their intuitive guidance, and experience the magic of life through ceremony, positive intention, and a creative, curious spirit. She lives in the beautiful Blue Ridge Mountains of North Carolina with her husband of twenty-five years and her sweet retriever pup. She can often be found exploring the trails in Pisgah Forest with her dog or meditatively turning her pedals on the Blue Ridge Parkway. When she's not outdoors, Anne is passionately speaking, leading workshops, coaching, writing, or making art. To learn more about her offerings, see photos of the healing dolls described in this book, or to contact Anne, visit www.anneheck.com.

SELECTED TITLES FROM SHE WRITES PRESS

She Writes Press is an independent publishing
company founded to serve women writers everywhere.
Visit us at www.shewritespress.com.

Painting Life: My Creative Journey Through Trauma by Carol K. Walsh. $16.95, 978-1-63152-099-0. Carol Walsh was a psychotherapist working with traumatized clients when she encountered her own traumatic experience; this is the story of how she used creativity and artistic expression to heal, recreate her life, and ultimately thrive.

Rethinking Possible: A Memoir of Resilience by Rebecca Faye Smith Galli. $16.95, 978-1-63152-220-8. After her brother's devastatingly young death tears her world apart, Becky Galli embarks upon a quest to recreate the sense of family she's lost—and learns about healing and the transformational power of love over loss along the way.

Of This Much I'm Sure: A Memoir by Nadine Kenney Johnstone. $16.95, 978-1631522109. After an IVF procedure leads to near-fatal internal bleeding, Nadine Kenney Johnstone must ask herself if the journey to create life is worth risking her own—and eventually learns that in an unpredictable life, the only thing she can be sure of is the healing power of hope.

Patchwork: A Memoir of Love and Loss by Mary Jo Doig. $16.95, 978-1-63152-449-3. Part mystery and part inspirational memoir, *Patchwork* chronicles the riveting healing journey of one woman who, following the death of a relative, has a flashback that opens a dark passageway back to her childhood and the horrific secrets that have long been buried deep inside her psyche.

Tell Me Your Story: How Therapy Works to Awaken, Heal, and Set You Free by Tuya Pearl. $16.95, 978-1-63152-066-2. With the perspective of both client and healer, this book moves you through the stages of therapy, connecting body, mind, and spirit with inner wisdom to reclaim and enjoy your most authentic life.